Foreword

One of the most enjoyable areas of our work here at Eber & Wein is hearing about all the various backgrounds, lifestyles, and artistic ventures of our poets. Your letters and phone calls pour in, and we thoroughly enjoy conversing with each and every one of you. One thing that has become so apparent is how a love for poetry is not exclusive to any one group of people. Mailmen, teachers, farmers, construction workers, professional baseball players, first-graders, graduate students—we've heard from all of you, and the range of voices, talent, topics, and emotions is really quite remarkable. With conglomerate anthologies such as these, the true value is found in the collective meditations of poets from so many different walks of life who share in this one special, common bond. Because of Life's extensive demands today, people find outlets in all sorts of activities. Where some find release through physical exertion, the poets featured in this collection find it through exercising their mind, with words and metaphors as their key tools. In today's world, there is a great deal over which we have little control, often related to certain elements of our lives or, of course, how we have been affected by our grim economy. Through poetry, however, we regain some of that control because only the poet dictates the visions, ideas, thoughts, commentary, and opinions he/she wishes to convey, without boundaries or intrusions. On paper there is no limit to the liberties we may take and, unlike prose writing, poetry gives us the perfect excuse to enhance or embellish our circumstances—to personify our innermost triumphs and tragedies with images that beg to be versified. So whether you are a delivery man or a special-ed teacher, never stop your mind from giving way to these liberties; let your imagination run away with them!

John Eber Sr.

Pie a la Rhyme

I like pie better than cake,
Yummy fillings, crusts that flake,
Edges crimped or edges fluted,
Fillings firm or fillings fruited.
One crust, two crusts, or crisscrossed tops,
Crowned with meringue or whipped cream dollops.
Pecan, peach, pumpkin, cherry,
Banana cream, fresh blueberry,
Deep dish apple, chocolate supreme,
Sour cream raisin and Boston Cream.
French silk, lemon chiffon, and Key lime,
All easy to eat, some harder to rhyme.
Oh, see, would you say that a Granny Smith a la mode
Is the star-spangled choice for the American road?
But I'm all for a rhubarb; that's pie, not a riot.
If you've never, ever had it, you gotta try it.
I could share mine with you, yeah, I probably should.
I sure would if I could, but I can't. It's too damn good!

Bob E. Boldt
Minneapolis, MN

Friends

A person and another person,
what's a better combination to start a wonderful friendship?
I found that out a long time ago.
A friend is someone who cares when something is wrong.
A friend reaches out a hand when others have fallen.
I have three wonderful friends that are all those things.
Everyone deserves a friend, no matter what you have done or will do.
Having a friend when times are bad
is like knowing or finding out
the greatest thing that will happen to you.

Chelsea Dugger
New Castle, TN

I love to write poetry and sing. I love to hang out with my friends. I live with my mom and cat. My grandpa is also at my house all the time. My grandma died in 2006; I miss her very much. My friends inspired this poem; I'm always with them. They make me laugh and feel good when I am sad. My friends are crazy and outgoing and I love them. My heroes are my mom, dad, and grandpa. I also have a stepmother, and she is really cool.

A Parent's Moment

Come, my darling, and kiss my lips,
And put your hands around my hips.
Our little boy will grow up fast,
So we must let this moment last.
One day we know that he will go
To Paris, Rome, or Mexico.

Melissa Marie Snowman
Vail, AZ

The Smile on My Face

The world is black and white, or so they say
There is no color, no shade of gray
I see more than just good and evil
More than happiness and dismay
I see the shades of gray
This is where I am
This is where he is
It is not the lion and the lamb
Those around me see only black and white
Should I disappear without a trace?
I may have to because I cannot live without him
For he is the smile on my face.

Ashton Hazzard
Plymouth, MN

3

Try Not to Step on the Flowers

Try not to step on the flowers
When you walk across the Earth
Be careful cause they're fragile
Like life and death and birth.

Let them grow to color
Sway in gentle winds
Bring awhile an honest smile
To observant friends.

As you run the race, slow a bit, you can
Let your eyes realize the color flowers send
A gentle cheer to humans caught up in the hours
When you run across the Earth, be careful of the flowers.

Nathan H. Miller
Palm Bay, FL

The Ghosts of New Orleans

I, the evil harlot stand tall
I, the adulterous shall not fall

Thus you've branded thee my name
But it is I who will live out your defame

You are my master, my country, owner of me
For no other reason than money would it be

Corruption and law go hand in hand
While the blacksmith heats his incorrigible brand

You dealt me a sentence worse than death
Forever a man's whore with every breath

Bought and sold, passed around
Back then, the bayou wasn't even a town

We became mothers of women and men
Condemned by society for someone else's sin

Forever we're unclaimed moms of many
All for your greedy man's penny

So dear Frenchman, madam, and sir
We were dually punished without murder

So many of us innocent victims of you
Corrupt officials that sent us to the bayou

Blessed were those who passed on during the journey
Who were carelessly thrown overboard on a makeshift gurney

We were pawed and mauled, beaten and raped
For us there was nowhere to escape

The bayou was too wild for a woman to survive
So we chose daily whether to endure punishment or die

Chasity Larson
Crestview, FL

5

The Direction of Life

Take one day at a time,
You don't have tomorrow,
You only have today.
Yesterday is gone,
And so don't look back.
Today is the reason to live,
To give all you can.
Spreading love and kindness
Will help bring a smile.
Energy and determination
Will help your dreams come about.
Then when this day arrives,
You'll look forward to the new day
And all that will transpire.

Marlene Burdoin
Gold Canyon, AZ

My poetry speaks my feelings. When something in my life stirs a thought, I then find that I need to put it on to paper. Life can be troublesome, and we can easily lose direction. My two sons are finding this out. After talking to each of them, I had this thought about life and wrote this poem.

In the Eyes

At the Cleveland Museum of Art, I watched
a security man as I waited for you to come
out of the restroom.

This man, who is surround by the artwork
of the ages,

(one of the best museums in the world,
I was told by another security man,)

was looking out the window
into the courtyard below.

When I approached him to find out what he was
looking at, he pointed to the trees below, budded
and about to explode into their glorious springtime show.

This, his eyes told me, was his idea of art.

As I walked away, I wondered if there was a
yardman somewhere who, as he prunes trees,
dreams of oil paints, watercolors, and canvas.

William E. Hiser
Lexington, OH

Little Brown Eyes

Soft little locks
Wrapped around little cheeks
Big brown eyes
With a little voice that speaks

Tiny little fingers
With laughter all around
Exploring and discovering
A personality you have found

Beautiful smile that captivates
Makes my world turn
My life has changed forever
My heart began to burn

Gentle little touch
Grasped a hold of my hand
Finally in this lifetime
I finally understand. . . .

Amber Cogan
Knoxville, TN

Family Time

The holidays are a special time.
You always get a least a dime.
Family members come to spend
The holidays until the end.
You can eat a Christmas dinner,
And you won't get any thinner.
You can play a special game.
But everything will feel the same.
Maybe it won't feel quite right,
But you and your family are still tight.
Soon enough it will be spring,
And you will hear that special ring.

Jazsmin Washington
Oak Creek, WI

Home

The sun was shining and the breeze was warm,
an old man was sitting in his rocking chair.
He was dressed in flannel with black fingerless gloves.
He smiled and waved as cars passed by.
His wife was sweeping the porch with a grin upon her face.
She watched her husband as if he were a child.
With each car that passed, her smile grew.
He laughed at her beaming as she kept on sweeping.
"A clean porch means a happy home . . . I thought you knew."

Ashleigh Anne Bukowski
Bay City, MI

9

Zephyr

The singing of a summer breeze,
Winds wandering from salty seas
Are the vital breaths of life
Weaving weather frost and freeze.

Wild wolfen howling,
As with eerie whistling,
Evokes an elemental force
Flowing, blowing, christening.

This swift, ethereal kiss
Brings a transcendental bliss
From an ebbing breast filled with
The living air and will-o-the-wisps.

Scarlet circulation of succulent oxygen.

A highway for the butterflies,
Bats and birds within the skies
Sail below a stormy ceiling,
Purpled by the slow sunrise.

Precious invisible pressure,
As if from this dawning treasure,
Bathe my skin in ecstasy,
A gentle gust, a peaceful pleasure.

This heavenly draft will last
If turbulent tempests are surpassed.

The animation of creation.

Rich Fahey
Chelmsford, MA

Carrickfergus

Carrickfergus I roll your name off my tongue
I imagine what you look like, what you smell like
I asked my father where am I from
He said, Carrickfergus up on the lough
I asked, what was our life there what did we do
Farmers I think according to your granddad
Not fisherman, I'd rather be on the water, said I
Be a fisherman then. It's Carrickfergus where we're from
I wonder about you. If I have kin buried there
Would I find a relative with my eyes and my hair
What's it like in your winters, are they bitter cold
Are your summers hot, does a dry wind blow
Do your crops turn to gold as the summer wanes
Do you have a fishing fleet that heads to sea in the rain
Would I be welcomed in your taverns for a pint and a nip
Would you think me a damned Yank if I made the trip
Carrickfergus you were once my home
I did not choose to leave you I did not choose to roam
My blood runs with wonder, what's it like where I was from
I say your name. I roll it off my tongue
Carrickfergus what's happening there now
I'm so far away, you don't know me anymore
Carrickfergus I yearn for your shore

Terry Hamill
Bloomington, MN

My father had traveled the world extensively in a twenty-eight-year military career.
He regretted never having made it to Northern Ireland, which was our ancestral
home. That got me to thinking of my Scots Irish roots and so the poem came to
be. I sent the poem along with a letter to the local newspaper in Carrickfergus. The
editor wrote me back to tell me a bit about my ancestral home, and we have been
pen pals ever since. I live in Bloomington, Minnesota with my wife of twenty-eight
years, Joilynn.

Whenever

Whenever can endeavor in forever.
However, when the sooner is the better
for doing whatever is the whatever,
then it's all left up to the whoever
to do whatever and whenever
as long as it gets done
instead of never, especially wherever it will
better their forever
why-ever and however.
Whatever!

Rene Jean Charles
Green Bay, WI

The Beach

I smell the breeze of the ocean air
Taste the lemon and lime tea
The scent of sand and sea I hear
Salt and shells I wish I was there
Sometimes I envision you in my mind
The tide comes in and out again
Feel the water wash over my toes
It seems to me that anything goes
Somehow now I'm all alone
Wondering where my sunset's gone.

Vista K. Koller
Indianapolis, IN

Kyle Cramsey

If you would forgive me,
I would hope you would love me forever,
but Kyle, I know you
love Andrea more than me.
You tricked my heart into loving you
when you didn't love me back,
but on my part, I used
you heart for my own good.
So I could see why you wouldn't
forgive me; it was just a
temporary fix.
We messed with each
other's hearts so much that if you
don't have one feeling for me,
I would so totally understand,
but here is a secret, don't tell anyone.
I still love you in a way
no one or anything could change.
I will remember you on the day I graduate,
the day I get married, even if
it's not to you, even the last couple
seconds I'm breathing, because one of my
breaths is worth a thousand of yours.

Saleen Chioda
Firestone, CO

The Sweet Victory

The storms in my life have passed,
Oh, praise God! I'm free at last,
Free from trouble and strife,
The heartaches of life

My Lord has given me
The sweet victory
Over all my fears
He dried all my tears

The sun is shining now
I cannot tell you how
All I know is Jesus gave me
The sweet victory

I will praise His name, Jesus
For it's always the same, Jesus
It has power to set men free
In the name of Jesus
You'll find the sweet victory

Peggy Shubert
Buford, GA

Walk in My Garden

Come on in. Take a walk in my garden.
All your fears will be forgotten,
and all your dreams will come a-trottin'
down the paths all through my garden.

Come on, take a walk, my darlin', the day is warm and bright.
To see you walking here, my love, is truly a delight.

Have no fears of us, my dears, for we will never fight.
We will drop our petals to show the way
so you can walk all night and day.

Just watch our thorns and you'll be adorned, for none feel forlorn
once they take a walk in my garden.

If you'll sit with me beside this stream,
you will see just what I mean.

For this stream here, for you, my dear,
will bring true all your dreams.

David W. Windsor
Crested Butte, CO

Untitled

Roses are red
Violets are blue
I'm steady missing you
Never have I experienced so much pain
I've cried so many tears it looks like rain
Reminiscing on the days we had
and how you made me glad
no matter what seems wrong
They'll soon be gone
No one will ever be able
to fill that void you've left
in my heart
Never will I forget you
No matter what anyone says
you'll always be mine

Crystal Wagner
Lansing, MI

Red

Red is hearts on love cards in your deck
Red is your favorite pair of Nikes and Jordans
Red is the taste of juicy strawberries in a strawberry patch
Red is the smell of roses during Christmas
Red is exciting because it's a Christmas color
Red is the sound of red robins chirping during the summer
Red is friendship that stays together forever
Red is the power that lasts to the end
Red is the party dress that lightens up the room
Red is the fruit punch at your birthday party
Red is the blood that drips from a bad bruise
Red is the taste of a good candy apple
Red is the sound of a red racing Lamborghini
Red is the blood of Jesus
Red is that go-cart that you want for Christmas
Red is the stripes that stand out on the American flag
Red is that popping fingernail polish everybody likes
Red is that Cadillac CTS you should have
Red is the color of love from your family
Red is the color of strength

Diasia Bunkley
DeFuniak Springs, FL

Beautiful Clothes

Beautiful clothes that we wear.
Garments that express thoughts and feelings of happiness,
sadness, and joy.
Clothes that cover us, my, how they speak.
Expressing themselves of what is being said from within.
Clothes covering hidden feelings.
Fluidly being worn over our bodies.
Tailor-made with deep pockets.
Filled with all kinds of threads of many colors.
Garments of clothes are such covering
Being held together by these threads.
Dyed red like blood, righteous blue so heavenly.
Gold so perfectly.
Green growing.
White, so pure.
Yellow, so cautiously.
Purple, so royalty.
Black, brown, gray, and pink,
And all other colors used so graciously too.

Lady Rozena
Bear, DE

Free at Last

When I was young and full of myself,
I just couldn't appreciate anyone else.

I could not listen to sound advice;
My heart was hard and cold as ice.

But now that youthful years have passed,
I find my heart is free at last.

Free to invest in the lives of others,
Sisters and wives, husbands and brothers.

Free to love and love in return;
To give of my heart, for love is not earned.

The voices of those who have gone on before,
Are calling me now as never before.

The say in this life, there's more than just me,
I'm only a part of a vast company.

There's nothing I do just unto myself;
All that I do affects someone else.

Each day brings a choice; so what shall I do,
Revert to myself, or reach out to you?

I'll make it a point to reach out to you,
For life's greatest blessings occur when I do.

Rance R. White
Alexander, MD

Snow

I am snow, soft and white.
When the air cools
and the trees become bare,
you know I'm almost here.

I am snow, soft and white.
I gently come down all the way to the ground,
not making even the slightest sound.
I blanket the ground like a sheet on a bed,
and I am as soft as the pillow where you lay your head.

I am snow, soft and white.
The wind that I come with is not so nice,
it is as cold as the water that has turned into ice.
When you put us together, we make a huge storm,
and people go inside by the fire to be warm.

I am snow, soft and white.
When the snow dies down and the wind stops blowing,
the children come out with their smiles glowing.
As the children play and go sledding on me,
their voices ring with happiness and glee.

Breanna Kelleher
Tewksbury, MA

Flight

The birds fly so graceful in flight.
We look up—it must be near night.
Nature at work, feathers of red, yellow, and blue.
We try painting, but never reach that lovely hue.
We also fly up in the sky,
Always questioning, always asking "Why?"

Adele Weitz
Monsey, NY

I Was Free

Here I sit, prone upon my chair as loneliness engulfs my mind.
I then decide to take a trip out in the cold and blowing snow.
I dress real warm, then ride the sleigh up to the highest peak.
As I descend, the wind lovingly caressed my cheek.

The trail is smooth and my heart soars
as I glide down between the trees.
The sun is bright upon the snow,
a million diamonds passed me by.
What a lovely time I had.
Then I turn my head and see the wind still blowing,
the snow still falling, and I still sitting in my chair,
but for a little while, I was free.

Ruby A. Greenlaw
Calais, ME

Me

Can you love me for me,
all my faults,
selfishness,
and desire?

Can you not judge
who I am,
who you think I should be?

Can you accept
my idiosyncrasies,
my neurotic?

Will you hold me
when my arms
do not want to be held?

And kiss me
why my lips
can no longer be felt?

If your answer is yes,
my ears will strain to hear,
my eyes will yearn to see,
this person that understands
the beauty of my verse,
me.

Michelle Burgess
Gainesville, GA

Untitled

My dad was wonderful with all the love that he gave us
and the path that he showed us.
His philosophy was live and let live!
Be true to yourself and to others. He always respected everyone
and he was there when you asked for help
or when he saw you needed help.
My dad was tough, loving, helpful, strong, independent, and brave
up to his dying day. He taught us to be strong and gave us
the faith that it was going to be okay when he passed.
He would say that every night he prayed about everyone
and would fall asleep before he got to himself.
I cried and cried from the time my dad was told he had cancer,
and had only a ten percent chance of being cured.
Then he was told he was clear of cancer in February.
I was joyful with praise to the Lord.
I told my dad I knew in my heart that he could beat this cancer;
he was healthy and fit to begin with.
His will has always been strong.
He was clear for two months, then was told the aggressive cancer
had come back. I cried and cried. My dad was told this type of
cancer was very aggressive and would spread fast. He had two or
three weeks left to live. Dr. Phillips and his staff were wonderful.
Hospice came, they were wonderful.
We were told my dad was the healthiest, but the sickest patient.
He has walked tall out of each severe chemo treatment.
It was a hard last two weeks for my dad, watching him try to push to
be his strong-willed self and too tired to do the things he loved.
I cried through it all, but when he left us, I knew his pain and
suffering were gone. It gives me great comfort to know
he is in God's hands now.
I have many fond memories of my dad
that I will always remember and cherish.
His love and strength were amazing.
Dad, we will always love you and miss you!
Hugs and kisses forever.

Paulene Shukoski
Neenah, WI

23

The Finest Steed

I left the house that morning,
the rain was coming down.
I said goodbye to Utal,
I had to go to town.

No sooner had I got back home,
my neighbor pulled in the drive.
He said your horse is lying down,
I'm not sure that he's alive.

I ran across the pasture
and fell down to my knees,
for there lay my Utal
dead beneath the trees.

A mighty bolt of lightning
had come down from the sky,
and struck that big ole tree
my Utal was standing by.

As I lay across my friend,
my tears mixed with rain.
I wondered why God had took him
and left me so much pain.

Then I heard the softest whisper . . .
"I wish to ride the finest steed,"
so the good Lord took my Utal,
the finest steed indeed.

Jerri Lynn Forrest
Romayor, TX

My Rae of Sunshine

When I think of you, a smile comes to my face.
When I close my eyes at night, I can almost see your face,
and just sometimes when the wind blows,
I can almost hear your laughter.
No one know the pain and sorrow I felt when you died,
or how my heart broke in a place that can never mend,
and when I close my eyes, I dream of you coming back to me
full of love and life with your arms reaching out to me,
so I can grab on to you and hold you tight,
never let you go with the night.
You're the angel God created just for me to help me though life,
so you can help scare off evil and demons that are in my life.
'Cause you are my own personal angel God created just for me
with your arms reaching out so I can grab and hold on tight
'cause when I . . .
when I look into your eyes, or when I see your smile,
or even when I hear your laughter, it scares away all the evil
and the demons that want to ruin my life
and helps me make it through until the day I'm with you
again in the afterlife.

Judy Myers
Tahlequah, OK

Dance of Death

The clang of steel on steel rings true
Reverberating through my like a bell
The glorious dance of death ensues
I'm caught up in it like a spell

Circling in an endless round
The dancers prowl on steady feet
Adrenaline rushes, pulses pound
Drumming out a steady beat

On and on the battle goes
Thrust, parry, slash, retreat
Each dancer landing glancing blows
Until the lesser meets defeat

The victor sheaths his gory blade
The victim grips his bloody chest
To the devil, one more soul is paid
In tribute to the dance of death

Stephanie Loss
Fruitport, MI

Never Give Up

I remembered a type of quote people used to say,
But I never really understood it until today.
Life will only get harder from here,
I think about it almost every time I shed a tear.
I look back on the happy years I once had,
And I wish for them to come back oh, so bad.
Pressure is a big part of teenage lives today.
Temptation of sex, drugs, and violence never seem to go away.
You never really know which road to choose.
It seems whichever way you go, you're bound to lose.
Why does it seem like I can't smile like before,
As if the joyous part of me walked right out the door.
I never show my true feelings,
Which is why I'm writing this poem.
I guess my feelings are personal to me
And I'm too embarrassed to show them.
One day I'll find happiness again;
I just have to live my life until then.
And while I'm waiting just for that,
I think I'll give myself a pat on the back
Because I've come this far without giving up completely.
I'm trying to enjoy life, it's very difficult, believe me.
I guess that's the message I'm trying to send out,
To keep your head up when giving up on all you're thinking about.
Take life's punches right in the face,
And you'll see things come to you at their own pace.

Brittany Johnson
Reidsville, GA

An Angel Scorned

Perched upon his back, the heavenly wings
Resting within his conscience, a heap of things
With the ability to save and protect
The sincerity in his eyes earns worldly respect
Yet focus pass the iris into the soul
The aura surrounding his heart temperature cold
Cold and distant due to the past
Witnessing communities burned down to ash
Tries his best to promote the glory
But life, live, love is only part of the story
Along with the good resides the evil
In a world that shows different sides of people
Adultery, larceny, murder, deceit
Oppression by the strong to those who are weak
To prevent disaster, by those who kill
Fight fire with fire that leads to more blood spilled
Which leads to more agony, leads to more death
Leads to more ache within the angel's chest
But how can he stop the cries of millions
Only one thing, absorb their feelings
And carry the burden, be the right in the fight
Fiercely enter the dark, and bring forth the light
For eternity this goes on, and the world still torn
A face full of tears, the results of an angel scorned.

Michael R. Johnson
Bronx, NY

I Miss You, Mom!

It's hard to believe it's been a year,
you seem so far and yet so near
I long to feel your touch,
it's you I miss so much
Down my cheek fall many tears,
in my heart, I love you so dear
It's hard to understand why
not having you here makes me cry
You have taught me so much,
I hope I carry on that special touch
As a wife and mother, you were always there,
because that was you, you always cared
As a doting grandmother, your grandchildren were spoiled,
the love you gave them will never be forgotten
As a nurse, you were dedicated in every way
and you showed it day after day
The angel that visited when you were seven
is with you now in Heaven
It brings me peace knowing where you are,
my memories of you will never be far
I asked God to take away your pain,
when you went with Him, it was then you won the game
Why, I will never know and my, how I miss you so
It was all in God's plan and now you are safe in His hands

Chandra Hillman
Deshler, NE

Paint You a Picture

I'll paint you a picture you may admire
Small candles lit with flames inspire
Surrounded by darkness, this glimmering fire
Creates dancing shadows that do conspire

And as they move, they know quite well
The stage above on which dancers swell
Obtain ovations that would be fit for Hell
But this mysterious location, I'll never tell

Eyes remain locked and linger
As one viewer may raise a finger
Among one, a many swinger
The heavenly voice of a singer

I'll paint you a picture you may admire
The lovely imagery may take you higher
The performers treat you as their sire
Or would you instead call me a liar?

Trevor Volpe
Wallkill, NY

I've always had a special knack for writing poetry, but it always kicks in following my dislike for poetry as well. A teacher that I had in high school had a profound impact on the development of my English language skills, and I owe her a great gratitude for the tools she has given me to accomplish this publication. As for my inspiration for this work, I could say that the greatest source would be the striking views I see out my dear window, allowing me to peer into the Hudson Valley's banks of which beauty never ceases.

Underwater Paradise

A small version me,
gracefully weaving through plant and stone,
diving deeply to touch
a miniature, neutral colored shipwreck.
With renewed interest,
I explore the hollowed center,
considering the quiet solitude
of my fifty-five-gallon underwater paradise.
Black, orange, and silver angels glide by,
looking at me in passive wonderment.
A school of electric neon Tetras
rush past, barely aware.
A shoal of playful Corydoras come close
to tickle me with their barbels.
I swim to the aerated curtain,
and let the bubbles carry me up to the top.
This is my world of whimsy,
just as Alice had her Wonderland.

Trisha Lynn Pittsley
Oswego, NY

Me

Whenever I look in a mirror
and my self-image I see
I say, gee
I'm glad Mother didn't abort me.

Mary Miller
Belvidere, IL

Remember

When you think of me,
That's when you give back.
Everyone remembers.
Everything remembers. Everything, everyone.
You, us, our world.
These are decisions that make the vibrations.
The energy of you, and us. Our surroundings.
Beauty or blackness. Joy or empty inside.
We're not always wrong, we're not always right.
It wasn't meant to be that way.
How would we learn? Pain, the ache, heartbreak, the awakening.
To remember, to move.
Forward.

Billie Jo Baker
El Paso, TX

Star Gazer

Given up looking for you and there you are
Waiting for me, suddenly, unexpectedly,
Universally and naturally.

Whether it really is you or in the corners of my mind,
There you are, waiting for me.

Moments caught alone, to be with you,
Searching for you in the light or in darkness.
You shine for me, bright for me.

When I can see you, it's like a wonder I've never
Witnessed, nor will witness again.
You belong to me, connected to me,
Like no one, nothing else.

Even if no one else knows or is aware,
It will always be for all eternity just you and me,
Gazing back at one another.
Suddenly. Expectantly.
Universally and naturally.

Valerie Rogers
Polson, MT

A House Divided

You have so much anger,
but you say you love.
How can this be so?
Hate and love do not reside together.
It is like a house divided.
In which part of your body do you store the hate?
From where does the love come forth?
You are divided against yourself.
You are a broken spirit.
You need to heal the separation
of your soul to become whole.
You first need to love yourself
before you can love another.
The source of love is God.
Are you connected to the Source
or have you unplugged?
God is always there and available,
we just have to plug in
to heal the separation.
It is up to us—we have freewill choice.
God is patient and He is waiting.
We have a direct line to God.
All we have to do is open to His love.

Laurene Meronek
Hampton, IA

Tales of a Confused Heart—a Single Mother's Battle

How many times do they have to fall
When will the pain finally leave
It has been forever
And still there is something there
A longing for madness, a desire for the fantasy
I know it's not about him
My heart wants the image
The completion of a circle to make a whole
Even though things still rotate
And the world continues to spin
I still feel an emptiness that nothing can fill
One foot and then another
Each day is a constant battle
You must get up, you must move forward
No time to sit and waste
I can't stop to take a breath
One pause, one blink, one look away
Means that moment
Each tiny step
Every little laugh
Is one more milestone that I have missed
Because sorrow is all that I crave

Katrina Mayer
Post Falls, ID

Peace Is within You

Peace is within as I dream. I position myself to hope.
Without a sense of peace in my spirit, I find it hard for me to cope.
Today, problems have their own need, for yet they will not rest.
So you take life for what it has you and so you do your very best
until there is nothing left.
Every task is left undone
because the stress of this world will have you on a run.
I fantasize about happiness, for yet it seems so far away
because all I feel is pain and hurt in my spirit day by day.
It's kind of hard when bills are due,
but you don't have money to pay.
In spite of your enemy, who wishes hardship along your way,
a big smile is what I wear to cover up my pain,
yet a simple false grin is all there is to gain.
They say pressure bursts pipes; yes, this I do believe,
so instead of acting out in rage,
I gently fall gracefully on my knees,
crying for power and happiness, for only God knows His child's pain.
I also ask for courage to walk a narrow path
whether it's sunshine or rain.
I ask for the love to share throughout this world
so that every single thing I do should never be in vain,
and my sight is bright and open with sweet joy on my lips
to sing glory to You, old sweet Lord.
Glory is the praise for the wretched soul
begging for hope and peace so that I can be made whole.
Peace, be still among my spirit, I shall sing my praise to Thee
that all troubles will lose my spirit and my soul is made free.
Hope, peace, yes, deliverance is what I claim today and tomorrow.
With joyous praise, I shall sing glory.
His peace is in me, I shall sing my praise to our Jehovah
so that His kingdom will see the Master at work
as He brings out the peace and understanding that manifest in me,
a shining new star for the world to see.

Iris Thurmond
Augusta, GA

Snowflakes

High, high on a windy hill
I climbed so high, my heart stood still
And as I gazed at the scene below,
I marveled at the beauty
Of the new fallen snow
The tall pine trees moan and sway
Tumbling snow as I pass their way
To nothing else can snow compare,
Each tiny flake with its beauty rare
We could search forever and never find
In all that have fallen, two of a kind
Are we like the snowflakes from the sky,
Each of us fashioned by the Most High?
Do we tumble together without rhyme or reason
No matter the time, the place, or the season,
Or do we follow the steps of God's own Son,
Until for each our work on Earth is done?

Mildred M. Beeson
Cedar Park, TX

Potter's Clay

Like clay in the potter's hand, am I not in Yours
Imperfect, broken, waiting to be fixed and restored
Does it not all start with You
Then continue molding until there's a breakthrough

Like clay, I rest in Your hands
Willingness to express Your brand
Over the years through the pores of the clay
Took the wrong crossroads which led me astray

Now I come to You in need of repair
Knowing Your judgment will be impartial and fair
Like clay, hard until made soft
Use me, Lord, show Your craft

As clay in Your hands
If any scoffing, I can withstand
Broken, waiting to be fixed
From the clay that's premixed

For me an opportunity for a second chance
With personifications enhanced
So that all will see in me
A similar imagine of Thee

Annie Woods
Fairburn, GA

The Mischievous Boy

He was born on a cold December day.
His mom named him Matthew Ray.
When he was big enough to sit and crawl,
Matthew was always being mischievous and having a ball.
When he was six and he started school,
He didn't always want to listen to the golden rule.
When he was ten, he got a dog and named him Simon.
They would get on the four-wheeler and go riding.
Down the trail they would go with Simon on the back,
Matthew's red hair flying and his freckled face showing pure joy.
He had his friend with him and is a happy little boy.
Now that he has gotten older, he has a bigger toy.
He likes to run the Bobcat and other big machinery till dark.
Wherever he goes on the Earth, he will leave a mark.
Now that he has grown into a fine young man,
I know he has a good future which God has planned.

Frances Ward
Winchester, OH

When Love Walks Out

When love walks out
and another walks in
you think about things
that might have been.

Things undone
and words unspoken
feelings kept inside
and not free and open.

Another face, body, and heart
to replace the loneliness
that caused you to part.

Your heart cries out,
I love you and I'm sorry!
Too little, too late,
you've already found
them out on a date!

When you know what's happened
in the room they were in,
is when love walks out
and another walks in.

Steve Bond
Ardmore, OK

In the Wintertime

In the wintertime,
everything is beautiful when there
is snow on the ground, trees, bushes,
and shrubbery.

Janet Oelker
Lawrenceburg, IN

Day and Night

As the sun shines down on me
I look into the clouds
and think, what do I see?
When the sun goes down
the beautiful colors fill the sky
I think how fast the day went by
When the moon and the stars twinkle in the dark sky
I question myself
how did the moon's face fool me by the eye?
As the cycles go over again
I think with just a million blinks
I loved this day
Why not like it anyways?

Lacey Lapp
Billings, MT

The City

(And there was the city
reaching out of purple haze
into the blacker night.)

From high up here it was
Peaceful,
A twinkling downtown display
Shimmering like a cocktail dress,
Glowing like the fires we built
To roast marshmallows
On summer nights.
No hint of its power up here
No more than its caress
Changing the night
Softly at a distance,
Easing it into deeper neverness,
Singing ariatic melodies to twilight,
Basking in the glory
Of the night.

Rebecca Cavanaugh
East Stroudsburg, PA

The Rag Doll

There she lies—the rag doll
Torn in many places.
She's been passed around and thrown about,
Seen by many faces.

When she was young and beautiful
And treated well—with grace,
She never knew that through the years,
Her beauty would lose its trace. . . .

She helped to comfort and to share
With many a sad-eyed child—
Then she'd be abused and punched around
When someone got too wild.

But her spirit kept on going—
She'd bounce right back and laugh,
Then be dragged along and left behind
On someone else's path.

A little more torn and tattered,
A little more pulled apart,
A little more worn and shattered,
She gave with all her heart.

Linda Lee Chapman
Westwood, CA

Lay a Rose

When I die, lay a rose upon my casket,
Black as the lonely night, muted by cloud covered skies.
Place it face down
For the stabbing upon my chest,
And let it trace the scars left
Upon my weakened heart.
Haunting words, day and night,
Leaves fresh scars inside.
I lay there in agony.

When I die, lay a rose upon my casket,
Black as a regretful heart,
Of not at least whispering how much he meant to me.
Yet each night passes
Without disparaging news,
Relief, release.
Someone, I know, still loves me,
But tormented by the inevitable,
When the security blanket is ripped from my arms.

When I die, lay a rose upon my casket,
Black as the guilty conscience which fills my mind.
To look around me, as if out of body,
To see weeping sorrow pouring from my heart,
But knowing I returned that love every second I could.
Was it enough?
To be sure,
When I die, lay a black rose upon my casket.

Destiny Centers
Louisville, KY

Shining Star

Twinkle, twinkle shines a little star,
Up beyond the world she stays away from us oh, so far.
Did you know that when she shines, it's not for her, but us all?
Did you know that she shines brighter even when she has a fall?
Twinkle, twinkle, brighter than the sun,
She's the brightest of them all, our number one.
Have you seen her on a summer night?
She gives off the brightest, most intense light,
But do you understand why?
It's because she cannot cry.
Instead, she shows us her at her best.
She never stops shining, she can never rest.
She's the one that twinkles on even past dawn,
Even when no one is looking on.
That doesn't stop her she still pulls through.
Trying to show us that we can, too.
We never notice it, we never care,
But then one day we noticed that she was twinkling there.
We looked up at her shining self and gave her a nod,
"Good job" we said, and then we continued on.
But after that day, she began to shine even brighter,
For those few words made her job lighter.
And still now she continues to shine,
But this time she knows that we acknowledge her in our minds.
Yes, acknowledge her is what we do,
Because Mom, we love you!

Sandra Maas
Palm Desert, CA

Bad Boys

Really should know better,
Past years have set a pattern.
Fell only for the bad boys.
Stole my heart, love, and joys.

After each man I swear, I'll change.
Last bad boy, his name was James.
A type "A" break-your-hearter,
I knew it, yet was no smarter.

Do you relate? I'll bet you can,
You too fall for this type of man,
Yet don't despair, don't hide and mope,
Look deep inside yourself and find hope.

This poem, although simple,
Sends a message to the mournful.
Yesterday's rain can cleanse your heart,
Tomorrow's but our brand new start.

Mary Ann Shaner
Ellwood City, PA

You'll Forget Me Anyway

I'll go away from you
You won't even care
You only think of you
I don't have time to spare
You'll forget me anyway
My scent, my love, my pounding heart
You don't care what I say
I want to split apart
You can't say it isn't true
There's nothing left for me to do
You'll be dumped
I gave you one last chance and you blew it
You didn't love me, and I knew it
Dare you say we meet again
You don't care what I do or say
Just go, you'll forget me anyway
Why me
Oh, the heart of mine wants to see
I want to cry
But you and I can never be
It
Is
Over

Julia Mikutina
Henrico, VA

Bleed Reason

Sadness is held captive in a night filled with cries.
Bold, definitive lines crossed, and then held in place with lies.
Fight the broken ties that shattered my beautiful eyes,
building hurting, painful tears in a flooded enterprise.
Cradle my weary head in tired hands of steel,
so torn up by burn marks that live far beyond heal.
Relentless frowns that seal a disapproving deal
that I once cherished as a meal too filling to feel.
Pain so deep, every crevasse leads to my soul.
No relief spoken or untold in this endless goal,
enriched by my heart's black hole that screams but can't beat whole.
Devastation has taken its toll, winning the starring role.
Please let me feel, please, serene, nonexistent peace
that has kept me intact, to say the least,
that has helped bury the burdened beast.
Peace to dry the flood and rekindle the steel.
Peace to heal the scars that remind me, just once more, to feel.
To finally fall asleep, and pray for forgiveness
for indulging this meal,
for doing this to myself once again
as I lie awake crying, not able to deal.
No reason to feel, but to bleed reason for real.
As I fell to my knees again last night and cried for you,
when my last tear dried up, finally through,
I felt my joyful heart renew,
and for the first time, I captured hope
that one day, I could possibly get over you.

Paraskevi V. Vourtsas
Haverhill, MA

Take a Look

Take a look in the mirror; tell me, what do you see?
I see a very strong lady who looks so much like me.
From the top of her head to the bottom of her feet,
everyone knows my mother was so sweet.
I thank the Lord up above for giving her to me.
My mother was woman like none other.
Take a look, you will see the classy hats shed use to wear
along with the beautiful suits; you wonder why people would stare.
My mother was known for baking sweets.
People would come from all around just for her treats
(donuts, rolls, tea cakes).
Now that she is gone, she passed all of this on.
As I look in the mirror each day, I can see
the looks of her in me.
You will live forever in my heart as long as I live.
Take a look in the mirror, I want the world to see
you and I were meant to be.
I am without a doubt my mother's child.
Take a look.

Brenda Colbert
Vallejo, CA

Eyes That Shine

Eyes that shine so bright
I can't see their depth
A soul brighter than the sun itself
A heart beyond comprehension
I watch silently from a distance
How I long to be with you
You'd never give me the time of day
I stay isolated, heartbroken
Coming undone on the inside
No one knows how bad I hurt
I put on a mask of happiness and joy
No depression showing, no one seeing through
I wait for the day to show you how much you mean to me
But that day may never come
So I just watch you with anyone but me
I die inside, I come undone.

Sherri Gardner
New Palestine, IN

My Dear Mother

I know you're gone and won't be back
each day I start anew,
but comes the night I miss you most.
Our talks, the hugs, the comfort, in "I love you."

The Lord took you while you lay,
there, in that very, very deep sleep.
No longer will there be any pain for you,
by His side is where you will keep.

I was so afraid to lose you,
a six-month-old to raise on my own,
yet I know you've been there by my side,
making every house a home.

That baby has but grown now,
a young man as strong as stone.
I know now what it's like for your
child to grow and soon you'll feel alone.

I know you are watching over me,
and helping me with every stride.
I only hope that those eyes are
watching over me and filling your heart with pride.

I miss you, my dear mother,
and the wonderful times we shared.
I only wish we had more time,
and I could have been a little more prepared.

Nola Downey
New Lisbon, WI

Voiceless Cry

A voiceless cry in the dark
One heard by those who can't hear,
For the pain that's ripping inside
Is one that he can barely hide.

He waits for an answer
To his voiceless cry.

He sits in the dark waiting
For what he cannot describe,
Maybe a light to pierce the darkness
Or one to shake his blindness.

He waits for an answer
To his voiceless cry.

Night by night he wonders,
When will the day come?
Even with others, he is alone,
When can he find his way home?

He waits for an answer
To his voiceless cry

He still sits alone in the dark,
Crying to those who cannot hear.
Awaiting there in total fear,
Just wanting to shed a single tear.

He waits for an answer
To his voiceless cry.

Alex La Mere
Rockford, IL

A Day with My Dog

It's rare that you'll find him stretched out by the door
More often, he's with me trying to even the score
With those nasty old pirates trying to capture my gold
And to stand up to pirates, you've got to be bold!

Sometimes he must dress in his armor and shield
And when I'm in trouble, he'll run to the field
Where the battle is raging and the fighting is heated
It's funny how he knows just when he is needed.

It happened one time that T-Rex caught our smell
So we started to run but I tripped and I fell!
Just when it looked like all would be lost
My dog came along and showed him who is boss!

Then we must hide from the saber-toothed cat,
And run to escape from the vampire bat!

We're finally safe, so we stop for a rest
And that's when my dog's really put to the test
Because out of the swamp came a mean crocodile
Who looked really hungry and smelled really vile!

We wrestled that croc and at times it looked bad
But my dog finally got him and boy, was I glad!

Now the time's getting late and the day's almost ended
It's time to go back to the fort and defend it
From all the adventure there yet to be found
'Cause when my dog is with me, adventures abound!

Kim E. Ewing
Spokane, WA

A Penny or Less

I'm a penny or less and it's
a true story and hurts to say so.
It's brown and round on both sides
and so am I, but considered Afro-American.
It's made in the U.S. and so
I was born, not much to be proud
to see or find as a shiny quarter
if one was seen on the ground.
They throw them in ponds, sidewalks,
and famous wishing wells.
Oh, how I wish the well
was more than a fairy tale.
It will take many to equal enough.
To be worth anything, and people to not
turn the other cheek; if you go to them
with many pennies, they say, "No".
Oh, how I wish I could be worth more than
a penny or less even for a day.
A day of the famous penny, one will never see
as the one-cent penny deep, deep,
deep inside is an illusion of me.

Angelita F. Aaron
Jacksonville, FL

Untitled

There's a place in my heart
where Jesus will not part,
and the devil must beware
because he cannot enter there!

Now my soul has been saved,
God's Son is the only way!

He loves us all so much,
and He blesses with His touch!

This Earth that we all share
He created with great care!

So remember when you pray
to thank Him every day.

By His Word is how to live,
our sins He will forgive!

To God we will run towards
for Heaven's our reward!

His love we will endure,
eternal life He will insure!

Mike Vaughters
Belvedere, SC

You Know Me

Lord, give me rest from all of this mess,
You know my future and You know what's best.

Lead me and guide me in the way I should go,
Lord, You're the only One who definitely knows.

You hold the key to my future plans,
I know You'll walk beside me and hold my hand.

You know my heart and You know my soul,
This You have known from the days of old.

Thank You, Lord, for carrying me,
Because without You, I don't know where I would be.

Phronia Hackett Rose
Gallatin, TN

In Remembrance

Somewhere above these
Starry skies
A lovely place
Called Heaven lies

When we fade from
This earthly place
The Lord will save us
By His grace

And take us to our
Heavenly home
No tears no hurt
No more to roam

He shed His blood
On that ole cross
So that none of us
Will e'er be lost

Hazel Pluris
Paoli, IN

My Marine

The man I love is now far away,
But memories of him are with me today.
A letter in the mail I wait to receive,
For that's all I have 'til he's on leave.

I write and tell him what is new,
And try to cheer him when he's blue.
A prayer each day that he's not here
Is said in hopes to bring him near.

Until world peace is finally won,
And duty to his country is done,
Friends and loved ones shall not be seen,
Because my man is a United States Marine.

Mary Yanchis
Franklin, NC

Tears

Today I shed tears without end from within the fountain of my soul,
mourning my sister's death, for she had taken my mother's role.
My heart was pierced with excruciating pain
that my mind, heart and soul could not control.
As my tears rolled down my face, falling and watering the rose
I held tightly within my hand, fearing once I dropped the rose
upon her grave, it would be our last goodbye
for us upon this Earth till when for she was dead.
So with teary eyes and a shaking hand,
I dropped the red rose unto her grave,
which would entomb my sister's remains unto dust for eternity.
I raised my eyes unto the heavens, and there and then I knew,
no amount of tears would bring her back to life,
for the Lord had reclaimed her soul.
Only my tears remained,
rolling down my cheeks till He calls me to join us together again.
I'll throw this letter to the winds in hopes it will find you
so you'll know I need for you to dry my tears!

Ursula L. Bennett
Alburquerque, NM

I am a seventy-five-year-old emotional writer; emotions speak to my heart and soul.
My poem "Tears" is about emotions I felt at the time of my oldest sister's death. I
could not talk or speak at the time, but spoke and wrote through my pen, which gave
relief to my heart and soul. I'm not a person that has to think what to write. When
the thoughts come to me naturally, I write them down every now and then.

Dear Journal . . .

the dearest idol I
have known wanted
that idol be help
me to tear it from
thy throne and
worship only them.
Does the place you're
called to looks or seem
so small and little now?
It is great
in God is in it,
and He'll not forget He's won.
Help me, Lord,
to show respect to others,
love to others.
Always mind others
are created in Your image.
May your love
shine through my life and
bring praise and
honor to You.
Amen.

Brenda Edwards
Joaquin, TX

God's near; no matter how steep your mountain, the Lord will climb it with you. He will light your path in darkness. His hands will guide you through. There is really nothing in this vast world to fear. God hears all your questions, He sends the answers so clear. Have faith, my child, He teaches us in the stars that shine at night. Believe in Christ, your Savior, your world will be all right.

Not a Day

Not a day goes by that I
don't cry for the birds,
for the trees, and for the
kids that simply aren't as
fortunate as me
Not a day goes by that I
can't see how strange and
cruel this world is to me
Not a day goes by when I
can't tell that when I
tripped, I simply fell
I fell into a world so
cruel and so strange
I fell into a world that
clearly wasn't big enough
for change

Dee Dee Regev
Northridge, CA

Sister

We were separated
I was thirteen
You were six
We were both young

I was sent to live
With my father
Because our mother
Despised me from birth

I missed you very much
And worried every day
Praying she wouldn't hurt you
And make you cry

I grew up and married
Had babies of my own
So glad you learned my address
Thankful for the letters you sent

They were an answer to prayer
And filled with love
I heard you're an angel now
Sent to Heaven up above.

Ginger Hamiel
Elgin, IL

Honey, I Love . . .

Honey, I love when I wake up in the morning
and see your smiling face.
You kiss me and say good morning and we embrace.
You and I brush our teeth in the bathroom,
comb our hair and wash our face
as we begin a new day together in the morning.
Honey, I love when we look in the mirror together
and make funny faces at each other.
You make me remember how I acted when I was young.
Honey, I love sharing some conversation
and eating breakfast together in the morning
as the sun shines through the window.
Honey, I love that I'm happy as I see you smile at me
and share a special moment.
Honey, I love when we run upstairs together and get dressed.
We see who could get dressed first and play a silly game.
We have fun laughing and talking and sharing special time together.
Honey, I love making you laugh and smile
before you go to school and I go to work.
As we start our new day together,
I begin to think about planning my schedule for the week.
Honey, I love making your lunch for school in the morning
and I love taking you to school every day.
Honey, I love watching you grow up
and enjoy every moment that I am with you.
Honey, I love talking about your favorite sport, basketball,
as we drive past the park on my way to school.
Honey, I love planning on playing with you after school
and look forward to spending time with you.
Honey, I love being with you every minute of every day.
Honey, I love you. My life is complete with you.
Honey, I love that I have learned so much from you.
We teach each other new things as we spend time together.
You taught me not to take anything for granted
since life is precious.
Honey, I love my life with you
and I thank God every day for giving you to me.

Ann Marie Pamias
Staten Island, NY

Riley Trails

To see the sun and the sky.
To feel the wind against my face.
To know that if I die,
I will miss this place.

Out where the birds fly free
Or just be,
It's this place,
This place.

James Crispell
Holland, MI

Captured Butterfly

Captured butterfly, are you like me,
Imprisoned against
Your will, yearning to be free?

Captured butterfly, did someone
Clip your wings and make you
Become another imprisoned thing?

Captured butterfly, do you hear the wind
Calling to you, beckoning you in?
Captured butterfly, oh, captured butterfly,
We are kin!

Bonnie W. Rogers
Meridian, MS

Angel Wings

Soaring high in the sky
Like a bird
We wonder why angels have wings
God our heavenly Father
Gave angels their wings
We do not know why
Everyone has a guardian angel
When someone is near you
Do not be afraid
That is your angel watching over you
Be thankful to God for all He has done

Karon Tyhurst
Martinsville, IL

A Winter Song

I can hear the jingle of sleigh bells
and carolers singing
making their winter song

I can hear the dropping of snow
and the neighbors making snow angels
singing their winter song

Finally, I can hear my family
and I laughing and having a good time,
making our own winter song!

Marissa Sankey
Montgomery, AL

How Much You're Loved

For every star that shines in the moonlit sky,
I could never count them all,
But I'd sure try
To show how much you're loved.
If I could measure every ocean, lake and creek
To discover how far wide and deep,
To show how much you're loved,
To climb every mountain high,
And walk every valley low,
Still could never be enough
To show how much you're loved.
So my beautiful Mom, on your birthday,
I want you to know
Even if I could count all the stars,
Measure all the waters,
Climb every mountain and walk every valley,
There's still not enough
That I could say or do
For you to know
How much I love you.

Timothy Stewart
Indianapolis, IN

I Miss You

I was with you
For the last twenty-four hours.
I held your hand,
I watched you struggle
To take your last breath.

Now you're gone,
And I keep wanting you back.
The hole in my heart is stinging from the grief,
And oh, I miss you.

I want you back.
I want to see your face.
I want to hear your voice.
I want to hear another one of your lame stories.
I want to stop the tears
Flowing down my cheeks.
I miss you.
You were so much to me and this world,
Son, brother, uncle, veteran, father, and grandfather.

But now you're gone,
And I want you to come back,
But I know you won't,
So I pray to God for you to
Rest in peace,
Grandpa Allen Arley Austin.

Danielle Austin
Washougal, WA

God's Promise

I felt my baby move today,
Nothing but a flutter.
I knew that soon enough,
I would be a mother.
To see your face, to touch your skin,
I couldn't wait for our life to begin.
Nine long months and now you're here,
I shed a single tear.
I thank You, God, for every day
Me and baby got to play.
I only had you for a little while,
But every day you made me smile.
When the angels came and took you home,
I knew I would never be alone.
When I see a baby's smiling face,
It takes me to that special place
That I will see with God's good grace.
No more sickness, no more death,
Only our eternal breath.
No more pain.

Kelly Eddy
Mesick, MI

Maggie

I wake up each and every morn
With four little feet
Scurryin' across the floor.
Tail waggin' as I let her out the door.
She's my faithful little friend
I dare to love to the very end.
When I come home from a hard day at work,
There she is, always ready to greet me.
I pick her up and hold her close.
As she smothers me with her kisses
I know in my heart that me she misses.
When the days are warm and sunny,
We go our for a leisurely afternoon stroll.
She sniffs the ground as if to smell
Another stray dog or strange predator.
I smile as I gently stroke this small ball of fur.
When I'm sick and feeling down,
She comes to me and rests at my feet.
She looks up at me with those big brown eyes,
Consoling my heart, consoling my soul.
She knows she's loved and cared for.
And however long she may be with me,
She'll by my companion and most of all, my best friend.
This four-legged lovable friend,
I call her my little Maggie.

Dora Frueh
Fulton, MO

Silence

Silence is a killer, but you won't die
for there's a door or a hidden window
for you to seek deep inside
Many opportunities waitin' for your knock
so get the key and get ready to unlock
for there are many shadows waitin' to take your place
but this is something no one else can do
for only you know the way
Silence is a lesson to be learned
but only if you're quiet and listen
to the pain and the hurt
so don't be afraid of the silence
for it's your being achin' for reliance
Remember no one can complete you
for your very own silence
brings you the only truth
Deep in the silence of yourself
there you will find warmth, love, and so much help
Let the strength of your silence lead you to freedom
because that's where you can unleash all
your fears and conquer your inner demons

Ameila G. Ramos
Rockport, TX

When Death Shall Come

When death shall come,
And it won't be long,
Don't look for me,
For I am safely home.
When death shall come,
And it won't be long,
Don't look for me,
For I will be gone.
I'll be at home in Heaven,
Where death cannot enter.
When death shall come,
And it won't be long,
Don't look for me,
I'll be with loved ones gone.
At home in Heaven,
I know I'll be.
When death shall come,
And it won't be long,
Don't look for me,
For now I'm finally home.

Douglas B. Wright
Hillsville, VA

New Poetry Contest

Hey, just maybe I'm a poet,
And as yet don't really know it.
Perhaps my words won't show it.
Actually, I'm an artist.
"Artistic" in words?
To some that's absurd.
But I am an artist.
Not exactly the smartest, but
I am an artist.
Well, now, wait a minute—hand me a mirror;
There's a follicle in my nose!
Look! Look how fast it grows!
First it was one inch, now it's two;
Omigosh! How much longer will it grow?
A follicle in my nose!
(such prose)
Oh, I'm too embarrassed to see.
I'll just sign my name with the letter "P"
(You know, AKA Pinocchio").
PS: Give me the scissors, please
Before I sneeze!
Now where was I?
Oh, my, my, my.

Sharon Valencia
Spokane, WA

I am "just a mother" with two grown, wonderful sons, Mathew and Gilbert. My inspiration for this poem was basically the opportunity to express myself in words rather than my art. The few pieces of poetry I've done in the past are of a more serious nature. They've been tucked away in a drawer only to be brought out as an occasion presents itself to family and friends. So I say, thank you, friends, for taking the time to read this. "Gracias, amigas!"

A Mother's Love

A mother's love, so tender.
A mother's love, so true.
A mother's love, so gentle.
What can be better than
A mother's love?
Thank God for a mother's love.

Vonnia B. Proctor
Jacksonville, FL

Untitled

Loneliness is like a prison,
there's no escape
when people treat you like an outcast,
ready to cast you away,
not to remember you anymore
when all it takes is a caring
voice on the other end to say,
"Hi, how are you today?
Is there something I can do for you today?
Would you like to go see a play?"
Time is of the essence.
Hours and minutes ticking away,
not a word from a friend today.

Sharon Dayhoff
Bryan, TX

Our Cabin in the Woods

There is a cabin in the woods
not very far away,
where our family goes to retreat
from cares and troubles of the day.

You can listen to the chickadee sing,
watch the hawk ride on the wind,
or see the tiny chipmunks
scurry into their holes.

Just being there where it is quiet
does your soul good,
though there is no guarantee
things will always be as they should.

You somehow have a new outlook on life,
and you begin to understand
that somewhere in the universe
there is someone who really cares.

Laverne Jelich
Mellen, WI

Good Friends

Good friends, good friends
What would life be without good friends
Someone who's with you to the very end
That's what they call good friends
A friend is someone you can lean on
Someone to take your troubles to
A friend is someone you can talk to
Someone who will listen just to you
When the going gets rough, you'll always find
Good friends won't be too far behind
Good friends will always let you in
They'll stand by you thick and thin
A friend is someone who can be
Sad when you are feeling blue
A friend is someone who is happy
When things are going right for you
Although we sometimes drift apart
Good friends are closest to our hearts
We thank God who found a way
To send good friends to us each day

James C. Smith
Kewanee, IL

I've been married forty-seven years We have three grown children and eleven grandchildren. We are Christians, and this poem was inspired by our church family who are our best friends. We are a small church who loves the Lord Jesus. We help one another in all situations. Praise the Lord Jesus for all His blessings upon us and upon Calvary Baptist Church of Kewanee, Illinois.

Untitled

Think up something. Think it through.
Realize the purpose. The process entangles you.
Make a move. Every group has a mission.
Some become movements. Most go unstated.
Insidious shadows will cast doubt.
Turn your idyllic picture to a grim, displeasing mess.
Envision the future. Envision your future.
Reflect on your recent activities. No good or bad,
Just what works. Approach with a sense of wonder.
This day is completely unique, and all outcomes prove it.
Don't move around to look busy,
Move around when there is a reason.
Strong ideas motivate you if the idea is big enough,
it comes with its own structure, a kind of map for completion.
Your sensing undercurrents pervade a conversation.
Some will label you paranoid.
Later, the same people will call you genius.
Be kind to the familiar face in the mirror.
The one who has been there for you all along,
and will stick it out to the end. Find your lost bliss.
Reconnect with the playful, selfish child in you.
Face this head-on.
Your genuine compassion is in part
why you radiate in the hearts of others.
Attention and nurturing may be the greatest joy.
Take it in stride and shake it off.

Tristan Nunn
Vista, CA

Sand

The sun beats down upon the sand
and warms it through the day
as children run and laugh and
build castles as they play.

The waves come up to kiss the sand
and beckons it to come.
Come with me now,
now to a different place beyond.

The wind begins to blow
and the sand moves to and fro,
shifting, shifting
not knowing where to go.

The gentle rains come down
and cool the day's hot sun.
It brings a needed relief
as the night is coming on.

And now the elements have passed,
the sand settles down again
Another day has come and gone,
tomorrow, a new day begins.

Shirley Flatt
Hammond, IN

Misfortune

Sad tears we cry
when dreams are forgotten.
Lonely days pass
as written sorrows
of a businessman's life.

To let go
of happy tears
is to give in
to life's wondrous beauty.

But for a lonely man's heart
it is to give in

to the past.

Tonya Pease
Madison, FL

My Child

Sleepeth there, my child
Underneath the willow
Golden hair, complexion mild
Faith and trust thy pillow
Dream sweet dreams of pleasant things
As you lie upon the clover
Above thy head, the gentle breeze
Stirs the leaves
As God's angel watches over
Behind me lies a mountain steep
Yet untroubled sleep is thine
For such as I the heavens weep
To thee yet fate is kind
Choose with care the role to play
Want not the easiest part
Choose instead goals each day
That spawn a happy heart
It seems that God
By the miracle of thy birth
Has sent a bit of Heaven
To dwell here on Earth.

Charles Wooder Shaw
Crawfordville, FL

Images of You

Over the years
How our family has grown
Each of us married
Out on our own

Images of you
Reflect in our face
In our manner, our style
Our actions, our grace

Each of us showing
Pieces of you
Images we'll see
In our children too

So you see
The circle goes on and on
Growing ever larger
Growing ever strong

Debra Friese
Sylvania, GA

Pray for Me, Mama

Pray for me, Mama while I am gone,
I'm far away and I can't make it home
Pray for an angel from above
that will watch over me with motherly love
Pray for me, Mama, I'm all alone
A lot has changed since I've been gone
Mama, I'm here in a really bad place,
and I think I've fallen short on grace
Pray for me, Mama, you understand
the scared little boy inside the man
You said, "Be a good boy, kneel down and pray,
Jesus loves you, it will be okay"
I hold on tight to the words that you say
It's your love that keeps the demons away
My search for happiness has taken me so far
Sometimes we get caught up and forget who we are
Pray for me, Mama, sometimes I am bad
My mind drifts away and I think I've gone mad
I remember, Mama, all the things that you said,
the lessons you taught me run through my head
You said, "Live a good life, be a good man,
and when you get older son, you will understand"
"Praying, my son, is a lot more than words
When talking to God, son, you need to be heard"
So I'm praying for you son, I pray for us all,
I pray you are ready when you hear the call
The call that I speak of is not from a phone
It's the call of our Savior, calling us home
Until then, my son, what else can I do?
I've sent an angel to watch over you
I love you, my son, and I wanted to say
As sure as there is a Heaven, I'll see you someday
Rest easy, my son, I'm praying for you
Mothers are like angels and praying is what they do
Pray for me, Mama, and I'll pray too
Just pray for me, Mama, and God will hear you

Mark Amason
Fort Worth, TX

81

Memorable Moments

There's misting in the morning. Sunny skies by noon.
The meadow's full of clover all sparkly from the dew.
Butterflies and daisies pop up in fields and groves
The smell of orange blossoms now overwhelms my nose.
The birds are chirping songs I've never heard before
With melodies so pretty, I can't record the score.
The children now are giggling and running through the field,
Their schoolwork now is finished; their happiness fulfilled.
Blue skies are changing colors as the sun begins to sink.
The clouds, once white and puffy, are turning shades of pink.
The squirrels are scampering quickly. The dogs begin to bark.
Our supper's almost ready and soon it will be dark.
Our families love to visit and sit our under trees,
Recalling friends and moments while laughing in the breeze.
The children bathed and curled up are sleeping in their beds.
Their storybooks and prayers new echo in their heads.
The day for us is over. Our housework is complete.
We don our nighttime clothes and tumble off to sleep.
Our God, He never slumbers and He never rests.
He watches and protects us. We know that we are blessed.

Laurel Harvey
Avon Park, FL

I am married to a wonderful man. His name is Ben. We have a son named Jack
and a daughter named Dawn. I was trained in the fine arts of drawing, painting,
and commercial art. I worked as a sign painter for fourteen years. Presently, I
am a Montessori teacher in Sebring, Florida. I enjoy working with children. I am
inspired to write poetry from life experiences, nature, children, and our awesome
God. Currently, I am learning to play keyboard and write songs. That's enough
about me, may God bless you all.

Untitled

Will you remember me at the close
of a tumultuous thunder lying dance?
As the rainbow colors of remembrance
speak of our truth, our journey,
will you recall the sacred undulations
of our physicality as we greeted our
Earth Mother and Father Sky on that
cool winter solstice time?
Our glistening flesh became the
welcomed moisture into our mother's
mouth and womb.
Have you forgotten the eagle's flight and cry
on Grandfather's peak on high,
the sacred Chanunpa and her blessed prayers?
Be strong, take courage, warrior of flight.
Dance between the sacred spaces of the
spiral within the source of our soul journey.
Blessed I am to have been gifted
the essence of your laughter knowing
of your deepest pools of ebony
channeling Grandfather's name.

Michaela Buchinsky
Anchorage, AK

Jesus Christ Loves Me

J is for Jesus, the strength of my life, whom shall I fear.
E is for Eternal light of my salvation, You are always near.
S is for Savior, Holy Lamb of God.
U is for understanding Your Word shall never turn void.
S is for Salvation, Alpha and Omega, King of Kings and Lord of
    Lords.

C is for Compassion, now abideth, faith, hope, and charity.
H is for Honor, power, glory, and domination are yours to decree.
R is for Redeemer, righteous Father, we love and bow down to Thee.
I is for Infinite, unlimited, influential, and endless divinity.
S is for Suffer; You saved us from the world's iniquity.
T is for Trials, Tribulations; You are worthy of the name Majesty.

L is for Lord, Your loving kindness have You drawn men.
O is for Omnipotent, gracious help,
You saved Daniel from the lion's den.
V is for Victorious, conqueror of our sin.
E is for Endure; the gates of Hell did You condemn.
S is for selfless, You made whole the faithful woman who touched
    Your hem.

M is for Messiah, Jesus, the name we love to call.
E is for Everlasting Father of all who is above all, through all, and in
    us all.

Kim Rena Ransom
Batavia, NY

To My Grandson

There is a precious boy named Zak
Who started pre-kindergarten a while back
Who made his mom and dad real proud
Because he stood out in a crowd
He loved to draw and paint
Zak reminded them so of a saint
Zak always helped with his sister and little brother
Zak was like no other!
Then came the big day
The twenty-first of May
Zak wore his cap and gown
Never making a sound
Walking proudly with his classmates
To receive his first diploma
Congratulations on a job well done
I love you more than the world is big.

Bertha K. Sutton
Lower Burrell, PA

I am a mother, grandmother, and great-grandmother. I had three sons and was married for over forty years, but lost my husband to cancer. I have led a beautiful life and pray to God and thank Him for all my blessings and thank Him for His angels. I feel they are with me always. I have always liked to write poetry. I wrote the poem, "To My Grandson," by thinking about him and how he was as a little boy. Then I thought about how I could put it in words that would rhyme.

Yet a Mother's Love Will Always Remain

She gives of herself with anguish and pain,
birth to a child almost drove her insane,
yet a mother's love will always remain.
She plans her day with no end in sight,
knowing at the end of the night, a sleepy child she must fight,
yet a mother's love will always remain.
She cooks through the day for a family she must feed
even if she cannot fulfill her own need,
yet a mother's love will always remain.
She takes the cuts and bruises of life
while healing the one her child has suffered from life's knife,
yet a mother's love will always remain.
She teaches to read, she teaches to write,
she stays up to help with homework all through the night,
for an educated child is awesome in her sight,
yet a mother's love will always remain.
She may even face a time for her child with hardship and jail
because that child made a decision that did fail,
yet a mother's love will always remain.
She faces grief knowing life is but a leaf
with a prayer being her only relief,
yet a mother's love will always remain.
She watches her child, never grown in her sight,
begin this whole battle she had to fight,
knowing her child, too will be all right,
yet a mother's love will always remain.
Dark clouds come and dark clouds go,
yet a mother's love will always remain.

Derrick K. Henry
Oakland, CA

My Friend

My friend can lift up ten blue whales by only using his pinky.
My friend is always nice, and he can really stretch a slinky.
My friend can hit a baseball all the way to the moon.
It only takes five seconds and it will not come back soon.

My friend can throw a baseball a thousand miles an hour.
My friend never gets mad and he would never hurt a flower.
My friend can see the future, he will be mayor of our town.
It'll be like that for 100 years and I will be a clown.

My friend's a movie star, he's in every movie.
He's famous worldwide, and the words he says are groovy.
My friend can turn invisible and his name is Larry.
There's only one bad thing about my friend;

My friend's imaginary.

Austin J. Alder
West Pittston, PA

Family

Sisters, brothers, aunts, and uncles
Grandparents, parents, and kids.
These are the causes of many white knuckles.
I could be a victim of family,
But I choose to be the creator of
A great legacy.
What is family, who is family?
We are family!
People related by blood.
People related by love.
These are the ones who sometimes
Hurt us the most
Just because they know their host;
Host, I say in a kind, kind way,
But the word is so true,
But not to make you blue.
As the words flow, the tears and fears
Cease for now.
I love them all, from the drunk uncle
To the young cousins doing twenty years to life—wow
Only because they wouldn't betray each other,
Not as long as they share the same father and mother.
Family—you need them and you should be there
When they need you the most,
Because in the end, only they
May be true to the host.

Gwendolyn Decker
Pensacola, FL

Spring Has Sprung

Spring has sprung
And with it has come
A promise of sunshine and fun.

Flowers so fair
They fill the air
For everyone to share.

The robin with his orange breast
Sits on a tree for a little rest.

He sings his song
All day long
For all of us to get along.

Antoinette Domina
Staten Island, NY

Nothing Lasts Forever

A rose is a beautiful flower
But it doesn't last forever.
The sun rises each morning
But it doesn't last forever.
Youth is a treasure that we cherish
But it doesn't last forever.

Our life we must live
Death is inevitable.
Love, friendship, and memories
These things are what we need to share.
Let's make these things last forever.
The loveliness of your beautiful face
The sparkle of your smile
Let's make these things last forever in our mind.

Dorothy Thomas
Vicksburg, MS

Look at Me

Everything about my life
is written on my face,
and the reflection that I view
shows thoughtfulness and grace.

You see those wrinkles on my brow,
their expression somewhat stern.
I got them from some worry
and times of great concern.

The crow's feet by my eyes
came as I was unaware.
I was watching all the sunsets,
forgetting all my cares.

And these tired eyes have seen so much,
all God's creations too.
Beauty, like the sunrise
as it glistens on the dew.

My skin is lightly tan,
and weathered was the way,
even came some laugh lines
when days were full of play.

Experiences large and small
made me who I appear,
but my life is far from over,
come and look again next year.

Sheila Rae West
Richfield, MN

We Are Blessed

We are blessed with many things
from the day that we are born.
Everything is all brand-new,
never old or worn or torn.

We don't know what blessings are
when we are very young,
but as we grow older and more mature,
we start to learn where they come from

We learn to say grace and bedtime prayers.
We sing in Sunday school,
but as we get to be teens,
those things are not so cool.

As we grow older and learn to be thankful,
we remember that we are blessed
and have been all along.
We thank our Lord for keeping us from harm.

Be grateful each day for what you have.
Count your blessings from dawn to dusk.
Put your faith and trust in Him,
and He will bless you much.

Peggy Swan
Memphis, TN

Morgan's Feet

Morgan's feet are now so tiny
Pink and a little wrinkled too
But it wouldn't be very long
Before she's walking all around for you.

First it will be kinda wobbly
And hanging on to things
Then she'll be off and running
And oh, the joy she will bring.

Then it will be school
Boyfriends and driving lessons, too
Those feet will take her
To many new things to do.

But whatever the future holds
And no matter where she goes
I know without a doubt
She'll always love you so!

Debbie Burnside
Hawley, MN

I Slept Among the Homeless

My days were dark and empty
from this special lady that stole my heart,
causing me to sleep in a situation
more drastic than a bench in the park.
Teardrops fall from the pain and sorrow,
praying for food and shelter, hoping to see a better tomorrow.
The rain is falling heavy and it's cold outside,
my pockets are running on empty,
but I'm scared to beg because of my pride.
So I say, excuse me, sir, do you have a sandwich
or at least some change to spare,
or maybe somewhere I could lay my head or do you even care?
But as I walk along these streets,
trying to find a place to lay my head,
ashamed of my situation, I feel I am better off dead.
That's when I dropped to my knees and to the Lord I
started to pray,
please bring me outta this situation
and bless me to see a better day.
You see, it's so easy to point a finger
and put the blame on someone else
when I'm accountable for my own actions;
in reality, I did it to myself.
You see, life is a valuable lesson,
a lesson that needs to be learned.
I ain't the one to play with fire
'cause if you play with fire, you will get burned.
No, I don't approve of being on the streets
'cause I know for me life is much better,
but I have slept among the homeless
and among the homeless, we stick together.

Jeffrey Langley
Grimesland, NC

94

A Great Country!

Americans, God loves you so.
There might be things that will happen some more.
Our beautiful country on September eleven,
business was a little slack.
We pray that God will watch over our backs.
Some people are saying all kinds of things.
We will never know what people in this
world will think or bring.
God will never let us go.
On our money it says "In God We Trust;"
to look to God, we must.
People we are very brave,
we knew that so many went to their graves.
Americans, we had a great fall.
Americans, we will always stand tall.
We invite people from all over the world
to come and live in this great land.
We love people and are always helping Man.
Our great country place, we must continue to love and pray.
We must keep God in our hearts
so Man and God will never part!

Mary Bass
Decatur, GA

My name is Mary Wheeler Bass. I've been married to Otis Bass over forty-two years and have three sons, Clayton, Paxton, and Otis Bass III. I have a daughter-in-law, Antonia, and granddaughters, Chelsea and Alicia Bass. The fall we had in New York on September eleventh, Clayton came home from school. It was his birthday. He hugged me and said, "Why did it happen on my birthday?" I will never forget the expression on his face. Tears came down my face. I said, "I can't tell you why this happened, my son, but I know for sure this must be many people's birthday." I had to write about what a great country we have. Every time, my eyes would fill with tears. In July 2009, I saw the poetry contest. The words came and I put them on paper, cold paper that has no eyes to search me as I write. Thanks for your kindness to express my thoughts to the world.

My Angels

When I see my darling children asleep in their beds,
my heart is so full that I think it might break.
They are like little angels so innocent and sweet,
so beautiful to look at I can hardly sleep.
They smell like baby powder and lotion so sweet,
as I stand by their beds, I silently weep.
I have been so blessed, they are truly angels sent from above.
I thank God day after day for my four bundles of love.
To have them and hold them and love them all day long,
on good days and bad days, we all get along.
Now they are grown with bundles of their own.
My heart is near bursting, what can I say,
for now I have six more angels
to have and hold and to love each day.
I have more than enough love to give to them all,
but now I am waiting for two more that are small.
When all of my children are done with their broods,
I'll have a total of eight angels to have and to hold.
I will love my angels forever and ever. Amen.

Sara Fields
Mission Viejo, CA

I Gather

As I gather only thoughts for the day,
just like that, I was taken away
As I gather myself a little more,
I began to fit right in like never before
I'd rather not say how I was losing,
but I will
As thoughts gather in my mind,
I can feel them drill,
making sure I know of,
because I have nothing to hide
As I gather some sense of knowing to be my guide
As I gather my time
to pass it by peacefully
Thinking of only good thoughts of you and me
I gather you're no better than me
when you wanna be taken seriously
I gather you wanna be as real as you can too, you see,
and while looking, I gather and I gather all there is too obtain
with all the knowledge I could in hopes I'd gain
and as I began to gain
I gather and I gather till I can't gather no more
I scooped up with my hands and my mind like never before
Learning and being taken for real, yes, I'd rather
I'd rather be on the inside rather than the outside
of this world in which
I gather

Gloria McBride
Framingham, MA

Bittersweet Addiction

Bittersweet addiction, try to steal my life away
On all my weaknesses you play
Constant contradiction, with all I do and say
What an evil game you play . . . that you play
There are those that are near to me who live in fear for me
And all my self-destructive ways
Oh, God, deliver me from my own hypocrisy
'Cause I know there's no one else to blame for this shame
I cannot live like this anymore
I've forgotten what I'm living for
Curled up crashing on a bathroom floor
Take it away
Bittersweet addiction, try to steal my life away
What an evil, evil game you play
Oh, God, deliver me, is there any hope for me
I cannot face another day this way
Oh, Lord, take it away

David M. Meeker
Colorado Springs, CO

A Mother's Love Is the Best

A mother's love is beyond the rest.
A mother's love is from deep within the heart,
it's been there from the start.
No matter how far we are kept apart,
the feelings just seem to get stronger and grow,
which helps us get through all life's woes.
Just remember our hellos.
How I miss our special times from spending the day together
to talking on the phone,
to just enjoying a simple ice cream cone.
No matter what the weather may be,
my mother's the one who's always been there for me.
Whatever may be,
a wonderful mother you'll always be to me.
The times have passed and now are memories must last,
for the time has come to be the mother you've been for me.
Now you can see the mother's love you gave to me.

Carla Lee Ann Santillan
Modesto, CA

Untitled

I have broken your wings.
You will not fly away,
your beauty mine, my caged dove.
Shimmering moon.
Songs from your lips
belong to me.
You are my caged dove.

Donville Reynolds
Fort Lauderdale, FL

Haven of Peace

A haven of peace . . . tranquility
A haven of peace . . .serenity
A haven of peace . . . perfect harmony!
A haven of peace . . . contentment
A haven of peace . . . no resentment!
A haven of peace . . . relaxation
A haven of peace . . . meditation
A haven of peace . . . hour by hour
A haven of peace . . . love and power!
A haven of peace . . . so inspiring
A haven of peace . . . quite inviting!
A haven of peace . . . paradise!
There is a haven of peace in Jesus Christ.

Latonya Lynn Davis
Port Arthur, TX

A Truth I Never Told

I keep having this dream I'm floating on a painting.
I'm stuck in the ocean, and it won't stop raining.
The colors begin to melt, and ocean turns to green.
The sky becomes the water, and I'm stuck in between.
I have this fear of swimming, I have this fear of motion,
But I have nowhere to go, my paintings in the ocean.
The sun falls through the clouds, I watch it go down under.
I'm looking for some shade to save me from the thunder.
I never thought it would happen but from the depths of the sea,
You rise up to my level, now you're here with me.
I've never touched or met you, but it's your face I've drawn.
I'm wrapped around your knees, the rain is finally gone.
Amidst all of this water, it's my bones that make you drown.
It's my life that you breathe, so I'll keep you around.
I have this fear of learning, I have this fear I'll grow.
But you take me on a tricycle, headed home we go.
I see the road ahead, and you have no part.
I smile and wave goodbye, you race back to the start.
I wake up and I laugh, oh, it was just a dream,
But I'm still on a painting, and I'm floating out to sea.

Leah Gillon
Tenafly, NJ

101

You

An immaculate presence
To the world unknown,
So beautiful, yet serene
With all that's going on.
Uncontrollable collapse,
Struggling to survive
Anxiously awaiting
That moment of delight
With this convergence of reality.
I show you to you
A blind trusting passion,
So responsive and true,
Tender and strong.
You are the key to my soul.
An inescapable grasp
On my heart that you hold.
Deeply euphoric,
The impression you give.
The compassion, the affection,
It's for you that I live.

Derek Dominique Davis
Lexington, KY

Untitled

A day like this, it's just too tough.
Let's talk about it.
It's days like this when it's never enough.
One soul, a broken heart,
another in sorrow.
At night they ask God, will I wake up tomorrow?
A family struggling, but still torn apart.
They can't stop the hurting of their hearts.
Lay arms behind their heads,
exhausted and tired,
but can't get to bed.
Everything is crazy; Mom in distress,
one son angry,
another one depressed.
She asks questions.
In mind, they scream out the good,
scream out the sad,
scream out the hate,
scream out the bad.
Instead, put on a smile and hide
to later cry at night, hoping they die.
They want to feel nothing
to cry alone,
to never show the suffering.

Bianca Mora
Salem, MA

Confused

My knees start to shake
When you're in sight.
My mind is filled with wonder.
My heart with fright.
When will this feeling stop?
When did it start?
How can I listen to my mind
Without breaking my heart?
I'm so confused,
What should I do?
I can't think of anything
Except you!
Should I ignore you
Or just give it time?
I can't think straight?
My heart controls my mind!
What should I do?
Is it time for me to listen to my mind,
But I want to follow my heart.
My mind is twisted,
My heart is broken.
This is bad for my soul
I'm going to let you go.

Courtney Stewart
Houston, TX

Shadows of the Past

A prisoner in her own home
The candle flickering, casting shadows on the wall
Those shadows are all she's got, all that ties her to this world
Slipping in and out of consciousness, yearning to numb her pain
The sound echoing around her of the down pouring rain
She hears footsteps, could it be
Or is it just my imagination fooling me
All alone, so cold, when before him she was so bold
Staring straight ahead, the world around her was standing still
Who could do this to her for their own petty thrill?
The walls are closing in now, the door swings open wide
In he foolishly stumbles, not noticing if she is alive
Right past her he walks, saunters on by
This was the day that the love had to die
She didn't sleep to dream that night, consciousness haunted her there
Straight ahead she would look with a defeated stare
To God she would pray
For redemption's day
Knowing for these careless sins, one day he would surely pay

Caroline Condon
Clifton, VA

Thank You for Loving Me

For time spent at work eight hours a day,
Thank you for loving me!
For time spent doing side work all times of the night,
Thank you four loving me!
For time spent riding my bike when you wanted to spend time with me,
Thank you for loving me!
For times when I don't listen to you,
Thank you for loving me!
For times when we don't see eye to eye,
Thank you for loving me!
For times you put up with me when you're tired and want to rest,
Thank you for loving me!
For time spent with my boys,
Thank you for loving me!

Baby, I know you go through some things dealing with me,
so I would like to take a minute just to let you know
how much I love and respect you. Thank you for loving me!
Today is Valentine's Day and it's your day,
so let's do whatever you want to do!

Kendric Tate
Cleveland, OH

Fact of the Matter

Talking about pollution is no fun.
Living in it is worse.
So before you dump it down the drain,
Or spray it on the land, think!
There are people that don't care.
There are people who do things some of us
Would never dare
To contaminate our food, our air.
We let them do it and that's a fact!
We must stand, we must fight,
Good food, good air, are our God-given right!
But God also gave us a brain to overlook this vast terrain,
But now we have acid rain.
You say you pray in God's name!
You ask who is to blame?
It's you and I for acting so tame!
I'm against acid rain. Yes, I will complain.
If you think that they're concerned, honey it's
Money that makes this world turn.
So to make sure you have your way,
Watch where you spend your dollar today!
When they don't see your money rolling in,
Guess what? You win!
Together, there is still time!

Deborah Ann Hartz
Deerfield Beach, FL

A Best Friend

A best friend:
Someone you know you can trust your life with
Someone you know will be there for you, no matter what happens
Someone who will toilet paper someone's house with having
no real alibi and have fun getting caught doing it
Someone who will ride home with you at two a.m.
when you're drunk as hell just to make sure you're okay
Someone you could make inside jokes with all day
and call it your hobby
Someone who goes mud riding with you in an unwelcoming place
where you get stuck with no one to call
Someone who, when you try and fight them, you burst out in tears
Someone who is there for you when the boy of your dreams
breaks your heart
Someone who will scream out random stuff with you
just so you don't look stupid by yourself
Someone who will share her shower with you when you get kicked out
Someone who takes care of stupid drunk people when they need it
Someone who is there for you if the test ever says positive
Someone who will go to Waffle House with you and your new
boyfriend and a group of close crazy friends who aren't always there
for you
but most importantly, someone you can call your best friend.

Courtney Brackett
Saucier, MS

Will I?

Will I remember when I'm old all that I know now?
Will I be able to meditate?
Will I still know how?
Will I be happy?
Will I remember to pray?
Will I take care of my soul for that glorious day?
Will I continue to be blessed by God with good health until the end?
Will I be able to suffer something while here on Earth for Him?
Will I still care about others even more than I do now?
Will I still visit with people and lead them to the Lord somehow?
Will I?

Ellen Labonte
Chicopee, MA

Alaskan Litter

Huge and ancient trees provide
Backdrop for this place where
Humans could, if they chose,
Live abundantly from sea and land.
We live a splintered testimony
To satellite dished-up media messages
Of consumerism.
Gentle deer wander through and
Ravens cry the morning at this
Playground where scattered excesses
Are noisy misfits.

Karen Farley Halverson
Nacogdoches, TX

Being Me

I'm not your typical female,
I grew up a tomboy, and I'm still one today!

I was as rough and tough as any boy in my neighborhood
could be back then. Everything the boys could do, so could I,
sometimes even better than them.

Growing up in a four-room cinder block house with my parents,
who were alcoholics, my father's mother, four brothers and one sister
with no indoor plumbing on several pieces of land,
along with the family dog, a collie named Peanut.

There were many times I felt like I was carrying
the weight of the world on my shoulders, like I was Superman
and could do anything I put my mind to.

I built a wall around my heart to protect myself from ever being hurt
and learned at an early age what I needed to do to survive
in the family I was born into.
Not knowing that you had nothing meant you did not know
what you were missing outside your backyard.

I know everybody struggles, and with my learning disability,
I learned to push through it and not let it hold me back.
As I got older and saw what the world had to offer,
I knew that I wanted to change the way things were going in my life
to reflect what I wanted out of my life.

Now in my fifties, I have accomplished many things.
I'm always there for my family and my friends when they need me.
Was a staff sergeant in the United States Army;
been in the war zone, now living somewhat in solitude off in the
boonies with two other Army veterans who are coping with a little
piece of mind away from the rat race of life.

Today, a United States rural route carrier for the post office,
trying to make ends meet. It's too early for me to retire from
working at any job that I do, so I must continue to move forward
on my journey to become the person I was always meant to be, me.

Bonnie M. Giddings
Traverse City, MI

The Life of an Addict

It's a long, lonely, and dark, deep path to nowhere.
To live by the thrill of a pill, just to heal.
It's your best friend and your worst enemy,
Yet to be your shoulder to cry on or in the bed you die on,
So try on and on.
Through the coldest of cold and through the darkest of dark,
My friends and family are still in my heart.
What I did wasn't smart.

Andrew York
Hulen, KY

At age fifteen, I associated with the popular kids, started smoking marijuana, got my driver's license, and a BMW. I had a perfect life and lots of friends. Then came the occasional use of harder drugs, then daily use. Before I knew it, I was addicted and my life became unmanageable. At twenty-one, I entered a detox center, where at night I would write what was going through my mind. I was proud when I wrote this poem. My counselor said it was great and hung it for everyone to read. I'm serving one year in the Bell County Detention Center, Kentucky, over drugs.

Grandpa and Me

I sit with Grandpa and watch the game
I don't know much about baseball
But he shouts and calls people by name
And jumps and makes a call.

I am just four, and Grandpa knows
I have to learn the plays
The home runs, the fly ball
And batting many ways.

He's taught me names
Like Wake, Jason, and Pap.
When he gets an out, I can shout,
Then I can wave my cap.

We have a good time,
Grandpa and me.
Mom smiles and says, "It's family."

Dorothy L. Darby
Hingham, MA

Family

Family is the greatest asset on Planet Earth
Family consists of our loved ones of unique birth
Family is so special and should always come first
Nothing or no one is allowed to disrespect our turf.

The growth of our family is a many splendid thing
With our natural bond and togetherness we're always stand
Our unity is strengthened when we delete blame and join hands
We have the most extraordinary family of the land.

Yonder there is Liberty Road whence we came
Our ancestors stood firm to save their land
As we feel the rich soil slip through our hands
History reveals what it took to maintain and gain.

Many years ago, our wonderful family name began with Mayes
Our persona of peacefulness is an amazing grace
Our proud heritage is from the African-American race
We'll take on the challenge to eradicate demons that we may face.

The gift of our spiritual family we love very much
Our concern for each other has a magic touch
Our treasurer of accomplishments exemplifies our stripes of us
We are solid as boulders and equally tough.

We are fair, we share, we care, and are heavenly blessed
We put God first and He gave us family to fill our empty nest.

Josephine Baumgardner
Richmond, VA

The Game of Life

Life is what you make it,
I've heard that's what they say.
You've got no time to fake it
'cause soon you'll fade away.
Life comes at you fast,
I've heard them say that, too.
There is no chance to slow it down,
no matter what you do.
Life is full of surprises,
some big and others small,
but you should try and take some time—
appreciate them all.
You can't live through your children
'cause they are on their own.
Your life is only yours to live
and soon they will be grown.
Try to tell them all you know,
except for stress and strife.
They will learn that as they try
to play the game of life.
Laugh and smile often
'cause no one likes a grump.
Embrace the days of sadness
when you are in a slump.
Emotions are the biggest part
of who you really are.
Hold them in and you can't win—
soon they'll leave a scar.
I hope this helps to get you by,
it's therapy for me.
It'd take three books of words to write
to tell you what I see.
Life is what you make it
but I guess it's all the same.
Remember me for who you see
and how I played the game.

Thomas LaClair
Danbury, CT

Days Gone By

Now I lay me down to rest
I promise You, Lord, I did my best
To tend the land for years on end,
I prayed the drought would finally end.
I drove my tractor and pulled my plow,
Broke pond water for my cows.
Combines, bailers, trucks and more,
I've done my share of a farmer's chore.
Sons once here to help tend my crop,
Now they're grown, that had to stop.
Farmer and wife now on their own,
A quiet house has become their home.
Through the heat and through the snow,
I prayed to you my crops would grow.
You helped me with my time of mourn.
Family members now passed on,
I'll see them again once I'm gone.
My father taught me all he knew,
His lessons helped to get me through.
Now renting out this land of mine,
I can leave some of my worries behind.
A new start to my life,
And home much earlier to my wife.
Bradford, Nunnenkamp, Estes, people everywhere,
Experiences, memories, filling up the air.
Then I hear a voice, speaking very fast;
Selling of my combine, my tractor, my past.
Sold to the highest bidder. Going, going, gone!
I look up and realize what is going on.
All of these memories have brought me to where I am,
A hard worker, a farmer, a strong, proud man.

Christy Myers
Hollister, MO

Flight

Reading a children's book, I dream
Whimsical sketches of a fairy tale
Just what is that butterfly's scheme
Laud to Peter Cottontail!

Broken shards of meaningless vase
Token cards in a stolen case.

A rabbit has always been mythical
Magic feet at their own sacrifice
A leprechaun has never been ethical
A key to the turret's gold entice.

Susan Reed
Wausau, WI

Why?

Why take my heart and allow it to break?
Why take my strength and my pillar away?
Why do I have to feel so sad and alone?
Why can't I just do as I please and have my heart stay with me?
Why, oh, why, oh, why do I have to feel this way?
Please make it stop, this terrible pain!
I don't ask "Why?" to be rude, disrespectful, or mean.
I just can't help asking you "Why" things are going this way.
Why, God, why?

Anthoinette R. Taylor
Jacksonville, FL

Rome for the First Time

Entering this great city with all of its fame,
The sights and smells as if I have been here before.
This feeling so vivid from my soul without shame,
These streets I have walked, of that I am sure.
Now the time had come, not wanting to leave,
With a hurt inside of me shouting silently.
My heart, heavy with sadness, needing to grieve,
Knowing I must return with an urgency so strong
To this city of Rome, where I knew I belong.

Amelia Piperis
Kennett Square, PA

Still Bringing Smiles

He was shy, but he could bring joy to make you smile.
When I was a small child, at Christmastime,
my dad would be so excited.
Just before dark on Christmas Eve, he would take a short drive
and come back home to tell me he saw Santa Claus
going into someone's house with lots of toys.
Oh, the joy of knowing that my turn would soon come.
In a rush, I put the milk and cookies out before I went to bed;
that was important to Dad.
And since I've grown up and had children of my own,
I still remember how my dad made sure
there was joy in our home at Christmastime.

Novella Davis
Evergreen, AL

Just Because

Just because I love you,
and want to show I care.
Just because I love you,
no one else can ever compare.
Just because I love you,
and know you love me too.
Just because I love you,
I'll always be true to you.
There is not a day that goes by
where I'm not praying for you.
There is not a minute that goes by
where I'm not wishing all your
hopes and dreams will come true.
So for every second, minute, hour
of the day, from here on out,
put all your faith and trust in the Lord,
and allow Him to work it out.
Just because I love you
and not afraid to let you love me,
but because you love me,
I'll always be here for you
just because.

Janay Thomas
Dothan, AL

My Hopeless Flame

My body worn to a dried crisp, limp with drawn-out fatigue
looking for something, anything, to guide me to a light.
Collapsing at rock bottom, I see a faint spark,
a chance, fate perhaps.
Though it doesn't appear stable, could it free my heart from prison?

The flame burned bright with time,
and freed my heart into a world of pure pleasure.
It provided warmth, nourishment,
and a seemingly endless amount of care,
resulting in security, confidence, conceit—happiness.
Never taken for granted, I cherished the flame
with all the love I could possibly give.

Until one day, my little light dimmed.
Only a smidge, but it darkened my world in its entirety.
I can't see! Where's my light? My guide? My angel?
No longer there, or so it seemed;
my life is purposeless without a light.

A sliver of hope, cuddling around the thought
of a slim chance of rekindling, I suffer.
The pain screams from inside me; I beg to you, let this be a dream.
It isn't. The suffering, the hurt, it's all real,
and far too much to bear.
I would much prefer my heart locked behind bars
than to drown in this sea of pain.

Lindsey McGovern
Reading, MA

Aunt Clyde

Aunt Clyde lived in a house out back.
It rose high above our little shack.
A tiny woman with mahogany skin,
A heart full of love and a welcoming grin.
That big old house kept calling me.
So many wonders were there to see.
Perhaps she'd open that old trunk today,
Or maybe she'd send me on my way
with a cookie she had baked,
A sweet that filled an empty space.
I always wondered what could be
In that old trunk she showed to me.
A beautiful dress for me to wear,
One that was new without a tear.
Perhaps some shoes that aren't too small,
They'd fit just fine in the fall.
Mama said they had to last
Until the last snowfall had passed.
A beautiful doll for me to hold,
Or a coat to stop the bitter cold.
I now know it was mostly junk
Aunt Clyde packed in that old trunk,
But to me it was all the things
I saw nightly in my dreams.

Joan Faulk
Gallatin, TN

A Warm Iron at Her Feet

You told me as a young girl a long time ago
You stared death in the face, but you did not know
Your dear momma was about to go
She just had my dad, your baby brother, only six months ago

She said she was cold, smiled and sighed
Your brother, Bill, knew and ran outside
You went and warmed an iron to place at her feet
At just sixteen, the gesture was so loving, so sweet
Trying to bring back your mother with a warm iron at her feet

Looking back on your long and well-lived life
You were such a lady, loving family member, and wife
I admired your accomplishments, sense of adventure, and style
Always gracious, religious, you loved to laugh and smile
Your natural harmony and beauty came through in everything you'd do
I learned to be proud, strong and independent because of you

But when I last saw you, my aunt, just the other day
Your gaze was already far, far away
Holding so many words you could no longer say
I was staring death in the eye, not knowing how to say goodbye
We squeezed each other's hand and I cried

So as I see you now in your peaceful eternal sleep
I think of placing a warm iron at your feet
Wishing to bring back my aunt with a warm iron at her feet.

Dona Elena Hatcher
New York, NY

You Had Me at Hello

You had me at hello
I know I heard you say
So how was I to know
This sunny November day
Would bring you my way
And totally blow me away
Your smile caught my eye
Enthusiastic and free
Your beauty shining through
As far as I could see
The beginning this was
On my journey to finding you
A feeling of love a desire to find
A need to know the love inside
The design of you the needs in you
The ways you love the desires you wish
Are the dreams we live
Is the reality I know
I knew the looking was through
The day I met you
You had me at hello too

Melanie Hanna
Kalamazoo, MI

Bathwater

If I were the water of your bath
I would surround you with mellow warmth
I would mold myself to every curve
And indentation of your body

If I were the water of your bath
Playfully I would roll on and off
Your satin and smooth body
With synchronized moves
I would gather myself in the
Recess of your navel

Then I would slowly, but surely run
Down into places only I dreamed of
As you release your sweet nectar
From my liquid love
You will always remember

That I was the water of your bath
As you reach down and pull the plug
You will know that I will be there
And wait for your naked return

Janette Brown
Oxford, MS

The Winning Hand

When the world seems a little cold,
just hold your head up and never fold,

because the hand that you have been dealt,
whether you're a woman or a man,

can only be unfolded by your hands,
for only you know what road

you've been down, and only you
know what hand you've been dealt,

so pick up your head and pick up your hand,

just like the cards that you deal,

and if you are strong and able
to play, keep on going,

because we only have another play
at life at its best or at its worst.

Only we hold the winning card within our hearts.

Jerdonna Senatore
Verona, PA

Mrs. Snow

How I love you so.
Your hair is white
just like the snow.

Mrs. Snow,

how I love you so.
You came from above
just like a dove
with love in your heart,
joy in your soul.

Mrs. Snow,

how I love you so.

Arlene Moody
Wildwood, NJ

For You

I would give my life
Not ask any questions why
Be there by your side
Hold your hand and understand
See through the pain
And hope to gain
I'll take away your suffer
To let you experience the other
I'll give you strength, aspirations, dreams
I will be your wings
For you, there's nothing I wouldn't do
Whether I say it or not, you know it's true
Not ask any questions why
For you, I would give my life.

Sarina Rodriguez
West Covina, CA

My Paradise

My paradise is in Heaven,
and no, I am not trying
to roll dice on the lucky seven,
or even on the eleven,
but know that my paradise is
in Heaven.

'Cause this world will be
left behind, and I pray
to God that it not be me
that will be left behind
with this crazy world
that will be destroyed.

My paradise is in Heaven,
and no, I am not trying
to roll the dice on the lucky seven
or even on the eleven,
but know that my paradise
is in Heaven.

I pray to God that I never,
ever leave His side.
I pray to God that I'll never, never
turn back again to that sin
I was once in.
My paradise is in Heaven,
and no, I am not trying to roll the dice
on the lucky seven, or even on the eleven,

but know that my
paradise is in Heaven.

David Yost
Hammond, IN

Flowers in a Jar

You always had flowers
Blooming everywhere it seemed
They were your pride and joy
I have pictures of them and me

I wasn't stealing that day
At your grave site
When I took certain flowers
At the time, it felt right

Maybe the reason I took them
Was because they reminded me of you
And the green thumb you had
Everyone knew it was true

No, I didn't need them
To remind me of you
I guess it made me feel closer
At a moment when I felt so blue

When I think of you, Grandma
Up in Heaven among the stars
I think you can understand
Why I have the flowers in a jar

Sharon Hill
Stuart, VA

A Spring Storm

I watched through the door as the skies were rumbling,
The clouds so low, so dark, the rustling of the leaves, silenced.
A siren in the distance, the stillness deafening.
On the horizon the clouds are hanging, Mother Nature is brewing.
I get a sense of fear, chills run down my spine.
The thunder is so loud, cracking, rumbling,
The clouds, they look so angry, resembling an ocean's fury
During a raging storm, crashing against the sea walls . . .
A loud rumble, no lightning to be seen,
The leaves, they blow ever so gently.
A tornado in the distance cuts a path through a city.
I hear the birds chirping, a sign the storm has passed.
What a delight . . . a sight, a sound, the smell,
How amazing life and Mother Nature can be.
Exciting, mysterious, like the signs of new life as spring begins.
In the air, there is a chill, a calmness all around,
I hear the thunder as it moves to the east;
The storm is over, there is a sense of peace.

JoAnne Wall
Thornton, CO

Soldiers

When you answered the call
To defend our country
You earned the right
Of our deepest respects
Words cannot express
The many thanks
That you deserve
For giving to us
Our many freedoms and liberties
May you always
Stand proud and tall
For being the
Bravest soldiers that
God gave to us all
Thank you for giving to us
Our many freedoms and liberties
Thank you for watching
Over our country
The land of the free
Liberty and justice
Thank you for the gift
Of being able to
Enjoy our many freedoms and liberties

Susie A. Workman
Man, WV

Lost in Translation

Sadness, loss, woes and sorrow,
Is there any hope for tomorrow?
Where has it all gone, how will it end?
Who do you trust? Trust no one, my friend!
Are you a believer? I hope your heart is pure,
for spending eternity in rapture or Hell is sure,
so choose now, my friend, for time will tell,
anguish or torment over peaceful bliss;
I wish you well!

Some say it's only our imagination,
but I want it to be my destination!
So much pain and heartache
I've found here on Earth,
now I want to know what it all was worth?
So I aim higher, my journey upward,
praying to end with a heavenly reward!
So come, my friend, don't put you life on rewind,
gain, take my hand, leave the painful Earth behind!
Don't worry if you accomplished anything while you were here.
The less you know while leaving, the better,
then you know there's nothing to fear.

Geretha E. Mack
Pinehurst, NC

I am a people person. I love my family, friends, and doing things to make others happy. I'm sixty-two years old, have three sons and four grandchildren. I've been married for forty-three years to the same man. On every job I've worked, and there have been a few, I was known as kind-hearted, giving, and gave great hugs. Love to send "thinking of you" cards to friends and family. I love to write; I've tried a couple of short stories, also poems, some not heard from again, none published. "L.I.T" was just in the moment. I don't take days to write. I write as I feel or see it, for example, "Holiday Blues." Some see Christmas as a depressing holiday with it fast approaching. I see what makes it that way! With the declining economy and crime on the rise, remembering Jesus is the reason for the season would be wise.

131

A Painful Smile

Where does this pain originate
What is left to contemplate
Why am I feeling so empty inside

Is there any end to this feeling
How very horrible I am dealing
With everything I've been denied

Smile, sure, why not
There isn't much else I've got
It's too painful to show

The wounds and the scars
Have been carried too far
Can you teach me how to let go

Deona Madrigal
Wichita, KS

Forever Today

This world of people going too fast
In a world that they know can't last,
Most never been in a world of the past.

Working at a saw mill,
Family's working in the field,
They were the backbone of America's will.

Didn't make much money,
Got bee stings to get some honey,
Had to eat the Easter bunny.

No electric, no running water with no bills to pay.
Just yesterday that turned into today,
Never will be a tomorrow, that's what they say.

Fancy churches, fancy houses going up all around,
People trying to put their roots down,
Will they need fancy when they are put in the ground?

A lot of children don't work, doing as they please,
Are they really living a life of ease?
Wondering if anyone cares or sees.

People scared, lost their jobs, don't know what to do,
Shooting people when they don't even know who.
What is this world coming into?

Elveta Crooks
Grayson, LA

A Pilot for God

I joined the ranks
During World War II
Air force my choice
A plane I flew.

God said, "You've served
Your country well,
Your fight for flight
Has been a spell."

He admired my courage
And gave me His hand,
"Rest now, Lieutenant,
Soar the lay of the land."

It had been awhile
Since I had flown
When God stepped in
And called me home.

My work on the Earth
No longer to be
He gave me wings
And set me free.

A pilot for God
A job to be done
Serving the Father
In my P51.

Julie Freese
Lander, WY

That Beautiful Woman

Once upon a time in Chicago, leaving my house after nine,
My eyes caught this beautiful woman dressed to impress, looking fine.
I guess she was going or coming from some place or another.
We still had the time to talk a bit and exchange phone numbers.
I said, "Let me go do what I do, I'll call in a couple of hours."
She said, "Take your time, my day is done,
I'm going home and taking a shower."
"All right," I said, "I have to go now,
I've got places to go and people to meet."
At that moment we parted, went our separate ways in the street.
That beautiful woman decided to become my friend.
I called her line, we made some plans to hang out and meet again.
I went to pick her up, she was standing there alone.
When I saw her, I almost died; she looked like a queen on a throne!
That beautiful, fine woman, what my eyes beheld, my mind raced.
A real true queen of beauty, strength, pride, confidence, on her face.
She didn't work to be beautiful, but she was,
And she was giving herself to me
I wanted to look in her eyes and see the beauty within
That only I can see.
I went to where she was, we stood at the door,
Like something made from Heaven above.
She gave me a hug, said something in my ear,
While holding me in the name of love.
"We don't have to go, just stay for a while with me."
I said, "I'll stay if you're sure it's all right."
My beautiful woman talked, I listened,
Then suddenly, she turned, I followed . . . off went the lights.

Bernard Williams
Memphis, TN

Seek Him

For those who diligently seek Him,
Our Heavenly Father is waiting to be found.
He listens for your calling voice,
and rejoices at its sound.
Since first written in His Word,
His promises are forever bound.
He grants my own petitions
Every time I turn around.
With every prayer He answers,
My faith rises to higher ground.
I cry to Him with thankful tears
As my mind His mercy does astound.
Praises flow from this joyful heart,
His throne they do surround.
With honor and glory as I worship Him,
The King of Kings again is crowned.
His name above all other names
Is worthy to be lauded and renowned.
His faithfulness lasts forever
For His children the whole world round.
So lift your voice and call to Him,
Letting your prayers upwardly resound,
For when you diligently seek Him,
That is indeed when Almighty Yaweh is found.

Trisha Brooks
Glasgow, MO

I Remember

I remember his eyes
Blue as the sky
I remember the way he held them tight
When they would fight
The way he laughed
At my expense
How he kept me safe
When he pulled me from the door
As the gunshot went off
The thing I remember most is
How his face is always in my dreams.

Annmarie Reddick
Phoenix, AZ

Inspiring Peace

A word of promise is said
A battle blossoms instead
Lives lost, countries clash
Power without blood will never pass
Selfish minds play the games of war and peace
Never-ending dreams great and small
Will never win, governments causing faults.

Sarah Patron
Oro Valley, AZ

Don't Go There

I was talking to a girl tonight
At her father's grave site
Asked her when he died
She got an empty feeling inside
Looked at me like she was dead
And said

Please don't go there
It's not that I don't care
This feeling stays with me
I hope that you can see
It's just not fair
So please don't go there

Everyone wishes they could just push "eject"
When someone mentions a touchy subject
They just turn away
And say

Please don't go there
It's not that I don't care
This feeling stays with me
I hope that you can see
It's just not fair
So please don't go there

Adam Riggleman
Fairhope, PA

Passing On

In perfect peace he smiled at me,
Ready now to go.
His time arrived, he whispered, "Yes!"
Reposed in Heaven's glow.

Eternal light filled the room
Bright in spiritual bliss.
As angels gently rose with him,
I felt his farewell kiss.

Lucille Irene Metz
Jenison, MI

The Abusive

Some people are abusive.
Some people think it's attractive,
and when they know that it's wrong,
they think it will make them strong.
And when they are doing things right,
they think that they won't go up to the light.
Every time that we get in a fight,
there's a fright.
But I can't stand
this horrified hand,
so I take this stand,
and I sit here and pray
till I live my last day.

Shelby D. Cook
Altamont, UT

One World Away

If you were far away, you could only see a bright, lonely sky.
The trickles of water rolling over the rough rocks
beneath the beautiful, crisp cliff.
Pine trees await the day they'll touch the vibrant, voluptuous sky.
But if you were to witness the breathtaking, exotic,
furious world of the decent unknown,
you'd see much more than any one human could ever imagine.
You'd see raving beauty. Divine islands behind the cliff.
We'd all see that there is a much more phenomenal world beyond us.
We'd see plum shaded skies with wisps
of tangerine and lemon through it.
An extraordinary beach.
Backgrounds of faraway lands, whispering in the distance
falling in time.
We hear the cries of the ocean,
the sounds of the wild.
We see the fine-lined detailed skies,
the God-given Earth.
We smell the scent of pine,
the scent of salt.
We taste the frigid air,
the dryness in our mouth.
We feel the rough sand beneath our toes.
The water flows through our hands,
and yet the most beautiful part of this
is the place that real beauty lies.

Heidi Wilkes
Baker City, OR

Pain

Pain is something you can only feel.
You can't taste or measure,
it's something that you can only experience and feel.
Pain can hurt you and can be different kinds of pain.
It can be emotional, mental, and physical pain.
Pain can happen from a cut and it can happen
if you get your heart broken.
It can happen if you get hurt.
It can be emotional pain if somebody breaks up with you.
It can also be emotional if you love somebody
and they don't love you.
It can be mental if you get put down by somebody.
It can also be mental if somebody causes you stress.
It can also happen if you get mentally abused.
It can be physical pain if you cut yourself.
It can also be physical pain if you fall down.
It can also be physical pain if you get beat up by somebody.
It can also happen if you fall off your bike.
So pain can be emotional, mental, and physical pain.
It can be emotional if somebody breaks up with you.
It can be mental if you get put down by somebody.
It can be physical if you cut yourself.

Sara Wiercinski
Erie, PA

Picture Me Rollin'

The time has come for me to depart the family I left behind
So hold your head up, and put on a smile
And just picture me in your mind

Riding my bike, or in the Lincoln, cuttin' the block, just strollin'
I know you can imagine that; if so, just picture me rollin'
My wife, sexy Mary, my daughter, Little Q, my son, Clifton T.,
You go ahead and cry for a little while, for again you will see me

I know you're gonna miss me, I'm gonna miss you too
Just have some faith in the Lord; mistakes, He does not do
You remember when we played spades, the cards I was always holdin'
I want everyone who really loved me, sit back and picture me rollin'

I'm Bro T from Atlanta, G, the words he would always say
But these words I speak from my heart, I'll see you again someday
I'll miss you, Vernon Keith Tillman,
Speakin' to people you did and did not know
Hardheaded, wouldn't listen to nothing we would say
But that's why we loved you so

I wish you could see where I'm at, the sky and water so blue
I'll keep a spot for my family and friends so they can see it too
I'll see you again, so don't you worry, sooner than you think
Your turn around and I'll be there, quicker than a wink

Let me go now, I've gone to rest, this body I'm leavin' behind
All I want you all to do is picture me in your mind
Picture me rollin'

Stephanie Moore
Brent, AL

I married Ralph Moore July 1, 1982. I have three children, Ralsheene, Ralph Jr., and Rakeem. I have two grandchildren, Kiara and Demetrious. I love to put my feelings on paper, so I write whatever I'm feeling at that time. That's how my poems come flowing from my pen. I've been writing since age six. I also write songs. I wrote this poem for my brother-in-law, Vernon Tillman, who passed away, and my sister, Mary. She asked me to write a poem for his funeral. I took what he loved and what I knew about him and came up with this poem.

Lovable You

You are the love of my life.
You take my breath away.
You set my soul on fire.
You are my one desire.
Without you, life is without reason.
You fill my every thought.
I love the way you look, I love the way you walk.
Without you, I will cease to be.
I will love you forever.
I hope you will always love me.

Judy E. Gray
Roanoke, VA

I am a divorced woman, college educated, living in Virginia. I currently volunteer at a local hospital four hours a week. I hope to publish a complete book of poetry in the near future. What inspired my poem was a friend I grew to love. I enjoy quiet times, movies, and a good book to read every now and then.

Through the Eyes of the Elderly

I look to you
My body shakes
My mind plays tricks
But I am in here
And I need respect
Oh I may forget things
But I still feel
I see you look at me
I feel your ignorance
When you rush by me or through my care
And I feel your frustration because of my "noise"
Or what you perceive as my resistance
But I feel
And I so want to tell you what I think
How I still feel though my words escape me
I was once you
Please see me
Help me
Care about me
Understand that I am still in here.

Shayne P. Marshall
Chester, NH

Ingredients of Self-Respect

I found the perfect recipe for self-respect
You start with two pounds of dignity
Mix in a teaspoon of modesty
Then add an ounce of sanity
Next you combine faith with moral and morale
A gallon of discipline is blended with determination
A sprinkle of grace is poured with passion and love
Dabble some trust with a leaf of perseverance
Later, pour in a dash of knowledge with a drizzle of education
Measure a quart of honesty
Pinch off a dice of loyalty
Followed by a tablespoon of hope mixed with strength
Then add a cup of righteousness and a grain of integrity
Sprinkle a piece of intelligence with a quarter of ambition
Add a drop of innocence with a bar of inspiration
Allow dedication and guidance to settle for a couple of seconds
Before you add selflessness and a dose of control
Use a dab of purpose and slowly add a helping of power
To water and dilute jealousy, greed, and too much pride
Apply a stick of courage to the mixture, along with confidence
Cut off a piece of obligation
Sprinkle a couple of seeds of compassion
Finally, add a slice of respect and let this marinade
For 365 days a year, twenty-four hours a day, seven days a week

Danielle Parker
Walterboro, SC

Broken

I wander alone in a large, grassy field,
Desolation as far as the eye can see.
Bare trees scattered, one here, one there,
Afraid and abandoned, just like me.

Windswept grasses part for my footsteps.
Somber gray clouds race over my head.
It's an ages-old vision of wind and sky,
Energy crackling and teeming with dread.

I can feel nature's power rushing around me,
My hair tossing wildly across my pale face.
But the pain in my heart is more overwhelming
Than anything here in this grim, dismal place.

I ask myself, how I can go on without you?
What did I do to chase you away?
Can I feel for another, or am I just destined
To think only of you, to keep others at bay?

You're a ghost in my mind, constantly haunting,
Darting and drifting, invading my soul.
Do you know what you've done, or have you forgotten
My very existence? Your loss takes its toll.

As the tears grow cold on my upturned cheeks,
I stop and stand silent, staring up at the sky.
The clouds move on toward the distant horizon,
And I'm left all alone again, wondering why.

Cathy Jefferies
Hamlet, IN

I Apologize

When I think of you,
I am reminded of the precious bond we've shared.
There was no limit to the pain you'd bear
to prove how much you cared.
You continued to support me even when I was wrong.
You were my comfort when life got rough.
You gave me the courage to carry on strong,
and I couldn't thank you enough.
I appreciate your dedication to remain by my side,
and I'm grateful for all that you've given me.
Most of all, I thank God for your creation,
because you are my "Statue of Liberty"!
The beauty within you is undisputed,
and your essence is everlasting.
The guidance I seek is in the truth you speak,
and you inspire me with each day passing.
Although we have our separate ways
and my mistakes may make up our part,
my love for you will never change because nothing
can take up the space you've placed in my heart.
I realize we didn't always coincide,
and I apologize for your pain and sorrow.
Know that I love you today as I did yesterday,
and I'll love you just the same tomorrow,
and although mere words cannot express the extents of my gratitude,
I need you to know that I truly do apologize
for everything I have ever put you through!

Johnny Carswell
Toledo, OH

The Wife of a Truck Driver

You hear people talk about a doctor's wife
who patiently waits for her husband to come home
after examining other women during the day.

You hear people talk about a lawyer's wife
who puts up with her husband fighting for
other women through the day.

You don't hear people talk much about a
trucker's wife who waits nervously when
she hears a truck wrecked on the news
until she hears who the driver was,
then jumps up and down
when she finds out it's not her husband.

The wife of a truck driver waits a week or more
for her husband to come home,
only to stay a few days; then it's time for him to leave again.
I know because I'm the wife of a truck driver.

Donna Stilton Sloan
Rocky Mountain, VA

Run Away

Let's run away and catch a plane
and fly into the blue
We'll fly for miles until we find
a mountain or two

Away from the ringing of the
telephone and people we must see
where nothing is scheduled for the day,
except for you and me

No squabbling children, barking
dogs, no salesmen at the door
No clock to set or bills to pay
no list of daily chores

We'll let fall upon our face the summer rain
for we know it will cause no pain
To talk and laugh about old love
and count the stars above

Let's run away and find that place
just made for you and me
and tell our busy world goodbye
for just a week or two (or maybe three)

Juanita Thompson
West Monroe, LA

My name is Juanita Thompson. As I write this, today is my birthday. I have been
married to my husband Richard for forty-one years. I have had heart surgery and
a stroke and my wonderful husband has been with me through it all. We have two
great sons and no one could have any better daughters-in-law. We love them as our
own. We have six grandchildren, five boys and one girl. They are our angels. I have
three sisters and one brother, the youngest two sisters being twins. They are what
inspired me to write the poem when they went to Utah to visit one summer.

Addiction

I remember the days when we first met, I was so naive and innocent.
In the beginning, I thought everything was great,
but soon that feeling turned to hate.
I thought I had found the love of my life,
what I really found was heartache and strife.
I fell in love with the way that you made me feel;
if I only knew then none of it was real.
I let you have control over me, a mistake I won't make again,
sneaky and manipulative, you were the worst type of friend.
You put up quite the fight, but now is the time to make it right.
So addiction, I'm breaking up with you.
I'm done with us, I'm done with you,
I'm done with all you've put me through.
I'm done with the guilt, I'm done with the fear,
with you I've wasted too many years.
I'll never be the same, you've caused me too much pain
and I want you out of my life.
I'm done with the shame and your sick twisted games—
this relationship must stop now!
Hour by hour, you're losing your power,
day by day, you're fading away.
It's time to move on, it's time to be strong;
this time, I'm taking a stand.
I won't let you take anything more from me,
my eyes are now open, I can finally see.
Make no mistake—with you I am through.
Addiction . . . I just broke up with you!

Shara Emmett
Royal Palm Beach, FL

I Don't Even Care

It's been weeks since we last spoke
Where have you been? What have you done?
Wait . . . why do I even care?
Laughing, I realize I don't.
You never had my heart,
we had a little fun—
nothing serious.
My new thing is going pretty well.
I know where I stand, there's no uncertainty.
I feel appreciated, important.
So . . .
thanks for the good times,
wish you luck,
"ciao!"

I wonder what you're doing now.
Maybe I'll call just to see.
No harm in keeping in touch with a friend.
Right?

Kerry Newbold
Centreville, VA

Otter Songs

I hear the otter songs
echoing through my memory
sharp and clear
as they did that day
from rocky perch to shore
at Point Lobos.

Watching their otter lives unfold,
I wondered how we, those tiny dots
moving clumsily along the shore,
appeared to those
sleek, dark beauties
whirling and twirling,
sinking and swimming,
diving wildly and gracefully
for those tasty treasures
hidden at the bottom
of that dark blue sea.

Jo Anne Riccelli
Minneapolis, MN

Breathtaking

As I stand here thinking of you,
I die deeper and deeper inside.
People may not see it on the outside,
but I feel it more and more each day
I have to see you, look at you, or even deal with you.
I feel like I am dying, but I now see
it's just love overpowering me.
So I just look and lay there, my face blue
and the last thing I get to say is I really did love you!

Carolyn Daugherty
Pearland, TX

I am eleven years old. I wrote this poem when I lived with my grandma. My grandma inspired me to write this poem by always telling me that I could always make my dreams come true and make them anything I want them to be, I should just go for it. So I did, I began authoring my own poetry. Now I live with my dad and have a special friend in Jenna Alemendarez. She is really cool and she helps me with everything. I also love canned cheese.

Complete

The morning light comes.
A new day appears.
Birds and squirrels are feeding,
Flowers and shrubs need water.
Grass and trees are growing,
A mailman delivers and smiles.
A cup of coffee completes the morning.

A phone call comes.
No one's heard from him since last night.
The whole world changed!
My baby brother has lost his fight.
We found him lying peacefully
On a blanket in his favorite chair.

He had such a zest for life!
So talented! So artistic!
He worked with paint and created with wood.
All the children loved him!
Christmas was his specialty!

He was a diabetic.
Legally blind, a kidney patient, and disabled.
It never slowed him down!
Always a front runner, always did his part.
He believed we could do anything!
But his life was obviously too short.

Peggy Kingham Prather
Lake Charles, LA

Against All Odds

You see, you can never be me
I have walked the road of true realities
Fought fights that only a winner can experience
Seen the precious lamb
Talked with God
Despite what Man has witnessed
Only to open my eyes and see my prayers yet answered
You see, I am living proof standing against all odds.

Tracey Holley
Columbus, GA

God Is with Us

God is with us,
He has not gone.
We cannot hide,
We cannot run.
He's with us as we sleep,
He's with us as we play.
God is here all night,
God is here all day.
So let's say His praise,
Let's sing Him a song,
For God is with us,
He has not gone.

Wanda Page
Wheatridge, CO

Love Me Once More

What happened to the days when you were crazy about me
When you were filled with the light of love?
I was all that you could think of
The fire burned bright in your heart then
It still does in mine, can't you see?
Your desire for me was strong
For your kiss and touch, I will forever long
Open your heart to me and love me once more
Let me feel the rapture of your love, which I so adore
Take me into your arms and hold me forever tonight
Let's unlock the mystery and our hearts will take flight
Hand in hand, we can follow the rainbow to our dreams
Gazing into each other's eyes, swept away by passion
Time without you passes by so slowly, it seems
As the flame reignites, our hearts will become one
You were my shining star, I wish you would come back to me
Open your heart to me and love me once more
Let me feel the rapture of your love which I want forevermore

Sonja S. Rodger
Sun Prairie, WI

A Brighter Light

Listen, my brothers and sisters,
To the wailing in a time of darkness so long ago . . .
A time of persecution and enslavement, a time of shame.
Many were held back, and yet many fought for freedom,
And now the wailing is not so loud,
And the darkness has some light.
As Martin and Abe and John and Bobby smile,
There is a new light on the horizon, a beacon for all;
A pillar, a light of hope in a time of continuing civil strife.
Many thought this day would never come,
But it has . . .
A triumph for the ages,
A leader of leaders in the free world.
Let us hope it will be a time of true change, a time of unification,
A time of binding up the nation's wounds, a time of healing.
Only then will the darkness of so long ago
Become brighter and brighter . . .
Not to be forgotten, but replaced with forgiveness and brotherhood.

Nancy Phillips
Christmas, FL

The Recession

The nation is at crisis as all prices rise
As high as the smog near the skylines
And when gas is like paying for gallons of milk
You swear you are paying for gallons of silk
Money evaporates like rivers in this heat
Soon enough, so will the street
Everything will disappear right before our eyes
As it all gets raised to the skies
And the sky turns black and burns red
It's screaming, "Help me, I'm dead!"
It is dead; it's missing a few parts
Because our emissions blew holes in its heart
Now we need an SPF of glass
Before long, we will need sun-proof casts
That we can't escape; we will never be safe
And us kids aren't even healthy enough to play
I need something to trust and believe
But not oxygen, the smog makes it hard to breathe
Simply when Alaskan temperatures hit 120
And when there's no value to our paper money
We all need a miracle and some magic
And as my watch ticks over the sound of traffic
I realize, we don't have much time left, all hope may be gone
But we will be all right if Obama stays strong

Deven Bora
Richmond, VT

Hello, readers, my name is Deven Bora. I'm probably not the average poet in this book, seeing as how I'm fifteen. This poem is really important to my life because I have seen my family struggle firsthand through the recession, and I really started noticing my poetic talent in eighth grade when we got a new teacher who brought us many new things, one of those things being poetry. She was a big influence in me writing whenever I could, and this is one of the better poems that I wrote.

Peace, Oh, Peace

Peace is only visible to the soul
Peace I get not from touch or sight,
For touch and sight bring me pain
Peace I get not from sound,
For sound goes silent when I need it most
Peace I get not from lights,
For light exposes my most hidden treasures

Peace I get not from nature, for nature surprises me with terror
Peace I get not from love, for love breaks my heart
Peace I get not from time, for time waits for no man
Peace I get not from dream,
For dreams shatter and die
Peace I get not from music,
For its lyrics are polarizing

Peace, oh, peace, where are you?
Your essence is beyond wealth
Your essence remains invisible to our eyes
You stop conflicts at their peak
Peace, oh, peace, I yearn to touch you
But you are only visible and perpetual in death

Emmanuel Wheagar
Parlin, NJ

Midwife at Midnight

The midwife went out of her small house that night,
She looked at red skies, then shut her door tight.
The winds of the Middle East blew the smoke high,
She smiled as she hummed a sweet lullaby.

She had on her long and familiar black shroud,
And humming and walking, she looked tall and proud,
But one thing was missing; would her courage fail?
Deliberately she had not put on her veil!

Her neighbors had warned her, "Beware if you're brave,
Or foolish enough to go straight to your grave!"
The midwife just smiled and said, "Quiet! You see,
I know that Americans take care of me!"

She walked a long path, then she stood very straight,
With no silly veil, she could deal with her fate.
She vowed on that night she would just burn her veil,
Even if it meant a stoning or jail!

She delivered a girl, she did her job well,
And her neighbors came forth with a story to tell.
They all said, "We're with you! Yes, our veils are going!"
And later that night, a new fire was glowing.

Mary Roberts
Las Vegas, NV

True Meanings

Happiness is hidden
Just between the lines
We all look so much better
When we're not underneath lies

Love is located
Somewhere between the lyrics of a song
We all keep everything inside
Just because we're afraid we might be wrong

Truth can be found
Between the hands of two
So many voices around us
If only I could listen just to you

Innocence is mixed in
With sadness and fear
We are all afraid of hurt
So we push always the ones we need near

Justice can be seen
When the nice guy finally wins
The one guy that helped everyone
Teaching that it's okay to let others in

So many wonders around us
If we could just open our eyes
Because good things come in small packages
But the best things come in disguise

Devon Gac
Troy, MI

I'd like to take these "100 words or less" to thank those who have made me who
I am. I would like to begin with my parents, who brought me into this world and
showed me the beauty in it. Next, my siblings; Adam, for always making me strive
to be a better writer; Andrew, for all the deep conversations; and Molly, who is proud
of me even when I am at my worst. Lastly, this poem is dedicated to my grandma,
who encourages and provides me with inspiration. This goes out to you guys!

If It Wasn't for Pictures

God took you back to Him.
Why? I'll never understand.
You are my gift from Him.
We are not supposed to take back a gift,
even the law says so.
If it wasn't for pictures,
I wouldn't have a tomorrow.
If it wasn't for pictures,
I would be drunk with sorrow...
If it wasn't for your pictures.

Irene Cotto
Hyde Park, MA

Vampire Strike

Shadow in the sky, leaves blowing on the ground
Moving too swiftly to even make a sound
Standing where you are, you better run for light
Because you are not protected in the midwinter night
Take a wrong step, they will swoop down in a flash
Struck down to the floor in an unexpected crash
Too brittle to move, with a backbreaking pain
A bite to your neck as your blood starts to drain
A little too much blood, almost close to death
As you let out a cry with your one final breath
You still cannot move as you stare at the sky
And he slowly walks away and leaves you there to die.

Jonathan I. Miller
Central Islip, NY

My Hands

I look at my hands, they look old and worn
I seem to age with the thought
They've served so many and worked so hard
At whatever life had sought

Have they done enough for my Saviour and Lord?
Have they labored hard at His task?
Have they clasped in prayer for the unsaved souls
With a fervor of love unasked?

Oh, Jesus, I pray, please accept these hands
Though aged, they are offered in love
Lord, by these hands, please lead me home
To Thy service in glory above.

Ruth M. Pittman
Orlando, FL

Babysitting Brouhaha

When he was physically younger and more "brittle"
Depion Saha was one of my two favorite kids who were little
That I hung out with day and night
Without having many a fight
We watched Nickelodeon TV shows
"Spongebob" is still my way to go
"Lilo and Stitch" were funny and cute
And no one of us could ever refute
The wisdom of the "Fairly Odd Parents"
Watching TV was one thing in which we were errant
Yankee ballgames made us want exercise and fun
My health was good then I weighed a ton
So we would attempt to fly away from the coop
By playing basketball hoops
For a while I did smile
But then Depion grew up and moved away a while
My health grew frail and shaky
And my bones "achy breaky"
I know keep in touch with Depion's mother
Despite the differences in our cultures
We had a friendship like no other

Dona Mary
Elizabeth, NJ

Dream Palette

The palette of my dreams
Exhibits varied pigmentation
Some dyes so compatible as to be fussed with at the seams
While others are considered an accidental mutation

If a hue appeals to the bearer
It will be pursued
The unused hues may be rarer
Dulling the love they once wooed

If bearers continue
To ignore the untouched pigments
It is then that they will truly begin to rue
As the paints dry out and lose their tints

Christine Kasparov
East Meadow, NY

Three Little Words

Three little words we so often use
From our head, our heart, our soul to express
In sickness or sorrow, happiness and bliss,
These three little words seem to serve the best.

With flowers, a card, a cake, and candy too,
Are usually most appropriate
With these words attached to.
Times there's no measure what these words can do,
To express it more freely, as shown from the heart,
These three little words that make no demands.

We are surrounded by these three words, you see.
Reach out and touch them, they may not come again,
And as you keep holding and giving,
Then it will surely not die,
These three little words, so simple and refined.

A genre for the choosing
To bind together mate, love, or friend,
These three little words,
There's never an end.

Forever to absorb shall stay within the soul,
These three little words, "I love you,"
I give to you, my very special friend.

Virginia Staley
Derby, KS

The Way of War

Listen,
and you can hear a country mourn
as ravaged by war,
its people hang their heads and grieve.
As every sight and scent of destruction
seem to merge with every breeze to become
a high thin wail of despair.
But it will not always be so,
for the day will come when those who
survive shall once more raise their
eyes in search of a future.
When the laughter of children will again
be heard across the patched foundations
and hurried graves.
But what of the non-survivors and the devastation?
The tears shed now for them will not soon dry,
but shall long remain a flowing wound
upon the consciousness of the country,
for such is the way of war.

Joyce Robertson
Browning, IL

Southern Breed

Born on a southern plantation
Tolling in the field from sunup to sundown.
Weary field hands on the way home
Can only talk about tomorrow,
Not actually knowing what life has to offer.

Growing up with cotton fields for your backyard
Summer sun, your straw hat;
Irrigation ditches, your swimming pool,
Not actually knowing what life has to offer.

Living in a tin-roof house
Trying to keep a roof over everyone's head.
Tolling from sunup to sundown
Just to make ends meet,
Not actually knowing what life has to offer.

All the children gone,
Lots of brighter days ahead.
Waking up at last,
Actually knowing what life has to offer.

Joyce Spencer
Lambert, MS

The Ben and Jerry Cycle

You realize you're missing love.
You need a kiss, you want a hug.
You find no man is available;
Now what you need is a drug.
You're running to the grocery store,
Searching for two men.
Spotting them in the frozen foods,
You look deeply into their eyes and apologize again.
Sitting at home with the two men on your lap.
The telephone rings—
A real man it brings.
He's calling for a date.
The date comes and goes;
You're in love down to your toes.
You say to Jerry and Ben,
"I don't need you anymore; I've found love again."
Months later, that male jerk breaks your heart,
You start to fall apart.
You miss how Ben touched you lips.
You miss how Jerry held your hand.
Luckily, so fast to forgive, those two men on that carton are,
You decide on buying ten, then means twenty men!
Smiling, you take them all home again.

Mary Loader
Brigham City, UT

Fantasy

Everything's perfect, everything's fine,
not wishful thinking, not a lie.
A bright sunny day all year long,
no laughing clouds to block the rays.
Smiling faces, tears of joy,
happiness flowing from door to door.
Stressless hours, worryless frowns,
only happy-go-lucky clowns.

Amy Meengs
Holland, MI

Innocence

Waters cascading down upon the rocks
Brush, alongside of a stream formed,
Animal life drinking to satiate its thirst,
Man as the interloper invades nature's privacy
Birds in the brush fly skyward to escape intruders
Insects immediately sound out their signal
That impending danger is now present
Animals bolt in fright as the nimrods approach
The enormity of what is to take place
For the pleasure of bloodletting
Has sent all forest creatures in seclusion
The stillness becomes eerie as each of its kind,
Like Man, seeks self-preservation.

Antoinette R. Goodlow
Union City, NJ

Be a Child Again

Where have all the children gone?
A long time ago, they were everywhere.
Encased in the plaster molding,
Reflected in the sidewalk mosaics,
And echoed in the chirping rhymes,
We marched forward into blissful history.
Our beliefs were dictated into existence,
While gathered beneath stained glass and steeples.
The pounding and shouting from the pit
Was a staple of the weekly covered dish.
As we descend with family favors,
So comes our innermost conceptions.
In the turn of a leaf, our lives are done
And our beliefs develop no more.
Our journey through disenchantment
Can surpass even etched emotions.
We must regress into our naive selves
To begin to grasp our place in eternity.
Woven amongst the sprouting branches,
We elate in our deity's supremacy.

April M. Standridge
Westminster, SC

Turn the Page

I don't want a heart that's hard or broken,
Nor one that's full of words unspoken.
It's hard to enjoy a moon so full
When inside you're empty except for the weights you pull;
When too many nights have passed by so cold,
While the only thing growing is your story untold.
When my silent sanctuary of steel and cement
Leaves my feet in the stocks with only room to lament,
When my wishes and dreams turn into sighs and tears,
And my days of hope turn into hopeless years.
While my eyes of fervor become dim with sleep,
And the word that saves me, I find hard to keep.
What happened, I wonder, to that girl that glowed,
When every moment she spent in heaven showed?
When suddenly that person you see in the mirror
Loses her sparkle, though the picture seems clearer,
What then do you do, my child of light,
When you can't go on or find the strength to fight?
You look to the sky and pray with your all
That you be filled with the faith that won't let you fall.
You pray for a heart that's neither hard nor broken,
And empty yours of every word unspoken.
You thank God from the depths of your lonely cage,
And find Him faithful as you turn the page.

Lacy J. Barnard
Hephzibah, GA

I'm in Love

I'm in love for the first time . . . again
My life started over with him
I'm on top of Pike's Peak
Too breathless to speak
I'm in love for the first time . . . again

I tried so hard not to give in
To Tom, Dick, or Harry, or Jim
But I was struck, what a jolt!
He's my thunderbolt
I'm in love for the first time . . . again

Lois Lindemann
Sweet Springs, MO

Exotic Flower

Your beauty is outstanding.
You are the only one standing
In my garden,
Which is my Eden.

Your incomparable petals
Open up your beauty
To the delight of my eyes.
Oh, sweet baby, you are so pretty.

Every minute.
Every hour.
Every day.
Every week.

I can't wait to see you
And smell the essence of you perfume
Until you're done blooming.
Wonderful, exotic flower.

Geronimo Aguirre
Salina, KS

The Greatest

The long awaited arrival of my creation,
built along the way is our foundation.
My life has never been more satisfying,
many memories are cherished and gratifying.
With each day that surrenders to the night,
for you, my daughter,
I will pass on my guiding light.

Shannon Kowalski
Rhinelander, WI

Autumn

Trees of yellow, orange, and brown.
Nature and beauty bound as one.
Rocks, hills, and streams of life.
Sunshine that smiles upon your face.
Another day, another night.
Moon and stars that blink good night.

Valerie Short
Klamath Falls, OR

My son, Nicholas, has been my inspiration for the love of his poetry and music.

Ode to Silence

The silence that is between heartbeats.

The silence of still point. That precocious fraction of a second where
a pendulum hits its high point and holds eternity in an infinite frozen
silence
before it moves back down again.

The silence between ticks of a clock.

The silence as large as the dot of a pin at the heart of the loudest
noise that was creation.

The silence of a forest with neither wind whisper nor bird twitter.
Silence so quiet it, forms a deafening roar.

Silence like the color black, absorbing all sound
as black absorbs all color,
to hide it until the prismatic moment it can be released.

Linda Jam
Roseburg, OR

Reflections of a Flower Girl

I remember clearly when I was only four,
This friend of ours came knocking at the door.

His name was Larry, he was my favorite guy,
When he asked to talk to me, I couldn't imagine why!

Now, I loved Larry, that I couldn't hide,
When he was around, I was always by his side.

He said he was going to marry his gal Sue,
And asked me to be in his wedding, too!

My little heart was breaking, I thought he was my guy!
There was a lump in my throat, I wanted to cry.

Would I be their flower girl? Yes! I jumped with joy!
Steven was to be ring bearer. Wow, what a boy!

Mom made my costume, it was a burnt orange dress.
Could I be good that day? It was anybody's guess!

When the big day came, I was as good as can be,
Scattering the petals three by three.

That's what they told me I was supposed to do,
But Steven, tired of waiting for me, sat in a pew.

The big day was over, what a crowd it drew.
If I had to lose my favorite guy, I'm glad it was to Sue!

Claire Webber
Billings, MT

Raindrops

The raindrops on my window reflect the teardrops on my cheek,
on lonely nights like these, I cry myself to sleep,
but when the sun comes out and the rain and storm has cleared,
on the inside I'm still crying, although you can't see my tears.

Christen M. Lewis
Milwaukee, WI

Soul Flying

Will you say goodbye
To the naked sky?
Dress the clouds!
Address those clouds
Come, say hi
Like the hippie guy
Claim to fly
Acclaim is fly!
The air up there
Thin as hair
Take this soul
Partake this soul!
I won't be shy
No more cries

John W. Bowers
Mechanicsburg, OH

Black Is Black

Black is the color of night.
Black is the dot in my eye.
Black is unappreciated and misunderstood.
Black is the forgotten thought.
Black smells like smoke from a summer grill.
Black tastes like the last remaining jelly bean.
Black sounds like a baby's cry.
Black looks like total darkness.
Black feels like the quiet of nothingness.
Black makes me want to sleep.
Black is the road to life.

David M. Brannon
Waldorf, MD

I Need You, Angel

The wings I see are tinged with gold,
Time is endless, or so I am told.
Feathery white, I know you're there,
In my heart, I know you care.
Over your shoulder, here we are,
Standing close, never far.
Wrap me up, envelop me,
I need you, angel, can't you see?
Shield me now within your wings,
Songs of joy we'll always sing.
Protect, love, and nurture me,
I need you, angel, can't you see?

Madison Ogima
Natalbany, LA

Can't Let Go

No matter how wrong things may
seem to be, you will always be
the one for me, and I can't let go!

When it seems like things are
coming to an end, somehow you seem
to let me know that I can't let go!

Even when there has been a long
separation between the two of us,
I yet know that I can't let go!

No matter what the circumstances are
and what people may say,
always know that I can't let go!

Cathy Carter
Philadelphia, MS

Legacy

Memories, there are a lot
I just don't know where to start
The stories that you told
As a child, I thought that you were bold
The life that you lived
There is nothing that I wouldn't give
To have been there, right by your side
To raise a large family like you did
You were very impressive to a small kid
To sacrifice like you did for your family and friends
You sacrificed right to the end
You have upon what you did need
But you did plant that seed
It grew as I got older
Now it flourishes and still gets bolder
Your legacy still lives on
In your descendants it will never be gone

Harley R. Criss
Sebring, OH

The Night Place

You are an unusual one
and some don't understand
the way you tend to wake at moonrise.
What is it you think about?
Were you there the day after everything woke up?
I bet you know these forests
almost as well as the one who made them.

Do you dream of the sunshine you never see,
and if you do, does it make you wish you could?
Are you wistful or content?
You must hear the gossip of those awake at day
picking and pecking at petty palaver
wrapped up in tight scarves of triviality.
Pay them no heed. You are of the night place.

The night place where matters are thought through
and questions are asked.
No one knows everything,
not even the moon.
The stars keep you humble,
but the trees keep you vast, don't they?
You are above and below.

Emily Hampton
Walkersville, MD

Untitled

A package came to me
It was wrapped in brown paper,
tied all around with an old brown string
and said simply, "Open me".
I put it on my table, turned it all around, and with a frown,
I reached out to pull the string.
I hesitated, I looked all around again; was anybody watching me?
I pulled and tugged, the string fell away.
I opened the box and there lay a locket shining so bright,
the chain long and loose laying in straw.
My mouth was opened in awe.
My mother had remembered me.
A locket given in love wrapped in old straw.
A tear slipped down my face as I remembered my Savior
had done the same.
A sweet babe nestled in an old manger, wrapped in old straw
had given to me a golden scepter to set me free.

Connie Rasberry
Tullos, LA

My husband, Huey, and I live in the little town of Tullos, Louisiana. I have written many poems and stories over the years for my grandchildren. These poems came from a voice saying "Locket" as I was praying; then the poem came so sweet to me. Poetry is so beautiful to me. I have six children and two of my brother's for a total of eight, and each one is a blessing to me.

The Visitor

I heard you call time and again,
But when I came, I couldn't get in.
The windows were open, I clearly could see.
Your house was busy; there was no time for me.

You were watching a movie that was rated R,
Your son and your daughter were fighting over the car.
Yet I knocked on the door and waited for you,
But you didn't answer; what could I do?

There was no doorknob on the outside, you see,
So I stood and I waited, hoping you'd come to me.
I waited and waited for a very long time,
But you had the TV and the phone on your mind.

You were too busy there in your home,
So sadly I turned and left you alone.
My heart broke as I walked away,
For you see, my child, your last chance was today.

Nancy Pratt
Big Sandy, TX

Children's Eyes

I took a star in hand and enclosed it,
cupping it in my hand, so I wouldn't lose it.

I opened my hand and alas, I thought I lost it,
but I looked into my children's eyes and saw every gleam
of brightness the star left behind.

Those inquisitive little eyes that shine brightly with glee
when they see you, eyes full of innocence and love
for the world around them, those are children's eyes.

Children's eyes are clear and bright;
they know not of hate, color, or language differences,
but merely look to everything they see in wonder and amazement
at having discovered something new to look at and love.

How I wish I could see the world through a child's eyes forever,
where there is no hate and only the thrill of new discoveries
that can only be seen through the wonder as seen by children's eyes.

Carmen Castillo
Uvalde, TX

God's Handiwork

Like a giant paint brush,
God makes the snow disappear little at a time.
Where there was ice and snow, now water runs in little rivers.
There are pink sunrises in the east.
The leaves are starting to show.
The air smells alive.

Like a giant paint brush,
God helps the warm winds sweep down the valley.
It makes the emerald leaves shimmer.
Flowers are blooming in an array of colors.
The perfume is being carried on the wind.
Gray thunderclouds build and rumble over the mountains.

Like a giant paint brush, God magically changes the emerald leaves.
Up in the canyon, the aspen among the evergreens are changing
    colors.
There are shimmering gold leaves and reddish brown leaves
Quaking in the wind.
The wild plum bushes are a blaze of crimson.

Like a giant paint brush, God moved the snow here and there.
Snow was pushed under fences.
It laid on evergreen branches.
In crevices of rocks,
It smothered picnic tables in the park.

Joy Butler
Riverton, WY

The Ballad of the Cat

A cat went on a walk
He could walk the walk
The only thing is he couldn't talk
Then the cat saw a cornstalk

The season was fall
The cat was by the mall
It was surrounded by a wall
That was being torn down by a wrecking ball

The cat decided to go to the park
There he left his mark
It was starting to get dark
Then he heard a dog starting to bark

The cat was very scared
He didn't know what to do
So he ran in the house of the woman who lived in a shoe
But the woman kicked him out

The sun began to dawn
But the cat began to yawn
Then the cat saw a garden gnome
So he knew he found his way home

Joey Ferguson
Warsaw, IL

The Silken Thread

Life is but a silken thread
On to which we cling,
Strengthened by our daily bread
At the end, there is a dread
To the beggar, to the king.
The thread's end, unknown, untold
But must be faced by all
Honor to strong, to great, to bold
Honor to youth, to time, to old
But all must face the call.
The time may come within a night.
The thread may break or end
So be prepared to see the light
Of death, of God, of Heaven bright
And from this life ascend.

Maybelle Belle Burgess
Seal Beach, CA

I was inspired to write this poem shortly after my husband passed away.

Far Away

Twinkle, twinkle, little star,
How very far away you are.

Away from the trees and grass so green,
Away from the seas of aquamarine
Close to the sun, close to the moon,
Far from puppies and colorful loons
Far from the flowers and mountains you are
Far from the cities with fast motor cars
Away from the people that laugh and play,
Away from the farmers out bailing the hay
You hold chats with the sun and
Talks with the moons
Have races with planets big as balloons
There you are, light years away
Yet you sparkle always by night and by day

How calm it must be to be up there
To be watching over all those who care
About how long it will take for you to come out
And flaunt your great beauty to all those about
How bright your shine is to be seen everywhere
To be seen by trains and by planes in the air
You shine on small children (that you do!)
From the UK and on to Peru!

Twinkle, twinkle, little star,
How very far away you are.

Samantha Beal
Knox, PA

189

The One the Storm Picked Out

I am the one that the storm picked out
To damage my mind with winds filled with the scream of agony
I am the one that the storm picked out
To twist and turn and make it hard for me to find direction
I am the one that the storm picked out
To make me cling to life and pray for my salvation
I am the one that the storm picked out
To tolerate the intolerance, the pelting rain of injustice
I am the one that the storm picked out
To stand strong like a mountain when the hurricane comes
I am the one that the storm picked out
To endure the tornadoes that ravage my surroundings and my
    familiar
I am the one that the storm picked out
To see it blow its course and outlast the winds
I am the one that the storm picked out
To see the rainbow He promised if I just withstood this storm
Thank you, storm . . . this rainbow, it's beautiful.

Rachel Coleman
Jackson, MS

What in the World Is Going On?

The good old USA is not the same, I fear.
All sacred, free, and established rules
Are now no longer clear.
We, the people, owned this nation,
Regardless of our wealth or station.
Mindless leaders cause aggravation.
Nothing is light in conversation.
Our money is gone, often jobs, too,
Foreclosed home? This mess hits you.
New ideas just hit the wall,
And if they stick, we hope they'll fall,
But they don't and we sputter and cough,
More bailouts, stimulus, and Bernie Madoff.
No one admits to another Hussein,
Their silence about that causes real pain.
Are there those who think he's Great?
Does their IQ float between five and eight?
We are told this happened before.
To get out of the mess, we went to war.
A war to end all, so what's remaining?
We can't deny our troubles are raining.
More rhetoric! Words, rarely true.
But we, the people, are thinking this through.

Hello, DC! We are out here by the millions!

Lois Jane Cleveland
Penn Valley, CA

191

Joy, Joy, Joy

Isn't life wonderful
With the devil and his cohorts in charge of the world?
He has a third of Heaven's angels.
Maybe they've multiplied; there are so many, like Noah's time
They are so busy "going to and fro in the Earth
And from walking up and down in it,"
And like "roaring lions prowling about, seeking whom they may
    devour,"
Creeping into houses to steal, kill, destroy, trade.
Isn't life wonderful
With the devil and his angels around in these last days?
The times will be difficult.
People will love only themselves and their money.
They will be boastful and proud, flouting God,
Disobedient to parents and ungrateful.
Nothing will be sacred, not even a marriage of a man and a woman.
They will be unloving and unforgiving, slander others,
And have no self-control.
They will be cruel and hate what is good.
They will betray their friends, be reckless, haughty,
And love pleasure rather than God.
Acting religious but denying His power.
This is—now!
Joy, joy, joy—Jesus, others, you.
Our hope—"I am the way, the truth, and the life!"

Janeann Moody
Wataga, IL

Dr. Thigpen

A true honest man
Became a fantastic father
Raised three fine men
The most thorough doctor I know
Is very caring
Pushes himself to the max
Admits when he's wrong
Has a gentle hand
We all shall gather
Always has a pen
Has helped many children grow
Even when it's a stethoscope he's wearing
Yet his services never lack
Should have a special song
Bring on a challenge
One he would take
This is Dr. Thigpen
What a wonderful doctor he makes.

Alice Stockner
Brunswick, NC

He's Western Kansas

He smells of fresh-mowed hay and leather,
Dry wheat chaff and dusty weather.
His cowboy boots and western hat
Are not for show; they're trademarks that
Explain his life, his love,
And like his Angus, he's a cut above.

Did his first climbing on a cattle pen.
Began riding the fences when he was ten.
He's watched his wheat and the top soil blow,
The pastures brown and the tumbleweeds roll,
The markets tumble; future plans crumble,
But with all the uncertain and all of the hurtin',
He'll be farming and ranching 'til the final curtain.

It's church on Sunday, in the fields come Monday.
Likes cattle sales and occasional auctions
Which give him a break from the
Calving and planting, haying, and spraying,
And fixing the fence on that dry creek crossing!

He's taken his turn with the wars of the world,
But he'd still volunteer to keep Old Glory unfurled,
For this is the life that he wants to preserve
To set an example for the rest of the world.

His handshake's a contract, his word, a guarantee,
He's western Kansas, and proud to be!

Jan Gantz
Ness City, KS

I was raised with a strong influence of the history and heritage of the West—the
importance of people, places, and events that explain who we are as a people and
exemplify originality, strength, and independence, pride and honor. That permeates
my life. I taught speech, English, and literature. Poetry is my favorite genre of all.
Like a musical instrument, even if the subject is dark or harsh, poetry can render
it tender and emotional with subtleties that create a picture with every word. My
publishing has been limited to our local paper and "The Territorial."

Norma and Jarod

Norma and Jarod, here I lay
Thinking about you every day
Your visits fill me with laughter and joy
Even better than Christmas with a new toy
I love her I love her with all my heart
I've loved her since the very start
She's held everything that's dear to me
My old clothes, toys
Even memories
There are a lot of thoughts I have for her
I can't even put them all into words
There is one thing that I can say
And stand by to this day
Is I'll love her, I'll love her for the rest of my days
Well, he's busted a few windows
Heck, broke down some cars
But he'll never put a dent in my heart
I find him to be near and dear
Even when he's drinking a beer
He's a very nice guy, as nice as tall
And I'll remember him as the best uncle of all

Estelle Mitchell
Eureka, CA

My Grandmother's Old Rocking Chair

As I walk into my grandmother's antiquated room,
I gaze across the hardwood floors
And observe my grandmother's old rocking chair.
It floods my thoughts memories and joy,
Of my grandmother rocking me
And telling me stories
Of days of old
Until I go to sleep.
When I awake,
My grandmother will still be rocking me
And telling me the stories about times long ago.
I look out the window
To see the fresh cut hay.
I say to my grandmother,
"Will you go out and play with me
For a little while?"
When we return to the old chair,
I would say to my grandmother,
"Tell me about the days long ago."

Nathan Gibbons
New London, MO

Inspiration for any poem, song, or life event is impossible without passion. For this particular poem, the passion may have come from cookies or apple pie while stories were being told. "For who among men knows the thoughts of a man except the spirit within him?" Corinthians 2:11.

The Redeemer

He came from a far-off land
To save the world and redeem Man.
Oh, my friend, what a joy it is to know
That His spirit can dwell in your soul.
He paid a price, you see,
He did it for you and me.
Seek Him while He is near,
And He will answer you, my dear.
Come, my Lord, come to us all.
To take away this dark, dark wall.
Exchange for the kingdom of God,
For you are the Savior and Lord of Lords.
Come to the east and come to the west
And save us from this trying test.
Come to the north and come to the south,
Don't let darkness take us out.
I hear the chariots of Heaven marching,
It is those angelic horses
Mounting up like eagle's wings,
And on one sits the King.

Mary L. Trapp
Winnsboro, SC

Wisdom of Lincoln

In the ages of our history,
I hear the wisdom of Abraham Lincoln.
"Don't turn me into a statue.
Just remember the Union. Do the work.
That will honor me."
Through storms and trials,
Lincoln says to me,
"Trust in that Divine being. Have a
place in making a new birth of freedom."
On wars: "They never make sense, but
freedom did not come without sacrifice."
On his assassination: "Don't reflect on tragedies.
Reflect on the good that is within you.
Always be charitable and have malice towards none."
On saving the Union: "There are many in
our Union who see wrong as right.
It will need the many who see right
to correct the wrong."
On John Wilkes Booth: "A disturbed young
man, but I am not bitter."
On belonging to the ages: "The winds of
time pass through years, but the ages of
history stand still, for those who study
will know their times will require of
them as it has done for me."

Bob DeLacy Jr.
Marengo, IL

Wasted Time

Time I wasted is my biggest regret
Time spent in places I will never forget
Now it's just me and hard-driven guilt
Behind a wall of emotion I have built
I am trapped in this prison, wanting to run
Thinking back on all the wrong I've done
The race is over, no place to hide
Everything gone, even my pride
Reality suddenly slapping my face
I am alone and scared in this horrible place
Memories of past flash in my head
Pain is obvious with each tear I shed
I ask myself where I went wrong
I guess I was weak when I should have been strong
I look to the past, it is easy to see
That what I was afraid of was to just be me

Melissa Evans
Crossville, TN

Ruse of the Proud

How tall the tree, straight the trunk,
Majestic, still crowned supreme,
Proud, regal to admiring eyes,
Yet vulnerable to inner rot, unseen.
Healthy bark, beauty deceiving,
Masks fractured pith within,
Silent breaks along fault lines
Are the portent of ultimate end,
The crash, the sham exploding,
The soul cracking at its seams,
Exposing what necrosed truth,
The dry rot in darkest dreams.

Robert E. L. Nesbitt Jr.
Martinez, GA

Leaving the Island

The monarch butterflies have left the island,
I watched them go—
A ribbon of flame unrolling low
Across the beaches
And scrolling 'loft like sunset in the midday sky
Raveling their way to Mexico—
The days are growing crisp around the edges.

Olivia Ferrarini
New York, NY

To Love Again

If you want me to love again,
Sprinkle sunshine into my den;
Where frost glazes my sunset days
Make dewdrops glisten in dawn's rays.
Rewind back the clock of time,
To when the prime of life used to chime;
Roll back the days of wine and roses—
Indelible images their memory rouses.
To bacchanal festivities, open the gate;
Usher in the nymphs, let me celebrate!
Perhaps love, guiding Cupid's dart,
May once again pierce this lonely heart.
In Aphrodite's arms, then I'll lull my pain
Knowing that I am in love once again.
But old and failing as I stand,
The game of love I once played
Wants no longer to hold my hand.
For a pilgrim weary and dismayed,
Withering and alone in his autumn days,
Friendship, alluring in so many ways,
Is my sole companion and consolation
Till I embark on my final destination.

Gomidas M. Jibelian
San Anselmo, CA

My Provider Is You

I know that You are my provider and everything that I say or do
is a direct reflection of You.
My desire is to esteem others in love, peace, hope and joy.
Being my best will glorify and honor You
as I continue to look up and not back.

Speaking life to all situations with confidence,
knowing that my needs are met,
I will continue to watch, wait, and pray
as my faith grows stronger each and every day
knowing my provider is You.

Juanita S. Golphin
Inglewood, CA

My God Almighty

Blessed be the Lord
my God and His cross
Thank You, Holy Spirit
now on to victory
against the world
the devil and the flesh
Men rule, but the
Lord, my God Almighty overrules
Thank You, Abba Father
In Christ Jesus' name
Amen.

Roger A. Nelson
Paterson, NJ

Please

Please, oh, please,
I don't know what to say.
All I ask
Is for Your love each day.
Oh, please, dear Lord,
Don't take away
Any more loved ones
In any more ways.
I wanna be an angel,
I'm an angel wanna-be.
When it's my time, I'd like to give,
If You'll let me, please.
Oh, please,
I don't know what to say.
All I ask You is
Don't take more love away!

Sally C. McKenna
Indianapolis, IN

Grounded

I dreamed I was flying
The ground below beckoned to my eager feet
while my heart reveled in weightless freedom
Experience told me to succumb to the invasive
embrace of this breathing earth
My heart, however, did not need a reminder
of the pain of vulnerability, of honesty
What is the difference in flying and being carried?
The wind feels no pain from knowing me
Transparency and invisibility are very different
I have been created for community and
nature tells me relationships are based on needs
It doesn't matter if I don't want it
I need to be held

Emily R. Chilton
Montreat, NC

Weaver

Weaver is Uncle Roy's garden spider.
Although she is not poison
I would not sit down beside her.
She weaves her web to catch her prey
And keeps it there for another day.
In the haunted house she saw
Old black widow hanging all alone.
She saw old skinny skeleton,
Looking for his bone.
She thinks it fell from his arm.
Weaver was not worried because
He could not do her any harm.
There was Mr. Whitey's ghost
Flying so fast, he hit a crooked post.
She saw Orangey, the toothless pumpkin
That didn't want to be carved anymore,
And not made into a pie,
That was for sure,
And the flying old vampire,
Nervous because darkness was about to expire.

Ruby V. Hyatt
Elmendorf, TX

Old Lady with a Cane

Old lady with a cane just walking along,
I hear you singing, are you going to town?
Say hi, passing by, the horse with white mane.
He will whinny hello, then hang his head down.

Old lady with a cane, are you new around here?
Where are you from, I've not seen you before.
The old lady laughed as if I'm insane.
Oh, I've been around, you thought me a bore.

Old lady with a cane looking lovely today.
There's a spring in your step, though you walk with a limp.
Are you well, can you dance, are you vain.
She wielded cane in the air, for sure not a wimp.

Old lady with a cane, may I make a request,
A favor, please? Don't take me to task.
Bring me some sweets from the shop on Main.
I'll be grateful forever. A favor for you, just ask.

Old lady with a cane, said "There is one thing."
Taking a moment to ponder, to beat him at his own game.
"Stop calling me old when it's you who is too lazy
To get your own sweets, and can't say hi to horse with white mane."

Marceline J. Engler
Hollister, CA

He Said

It's a cool and silent night,
When all the stars are shining bright.

Away to the heavens I look up high,
What's beyond that deep dark sky?

While everyone is tucked away,
I wait for the dawn of a brand-new day.

Suddenly, before I know,
The sun has arisen, oh, what a glow!

Tomorrow brings a smile to my face,
The warmest of memories I gladly embrace.

The season changes, the cycle turns new
Of wishes and dreams we hope do come true.

For no one knows what lies ahead,
But God is with us; "Trust me," He said.

Diann M. Farnsley
Panama City, FL

Change of Attitude

Kids stealing and killing in America
What has gone wrong these days
Many of them are out of control
They are selfish, rude, and disobedient to their parents
They have lost respect for themselves
Adults, their teachers, and authority
If they were not taught good behavior at home
It's hard to get it on the streets
Their conduct is very bad in school
It has become habitual
Instead of being a big brother to the smaller kids
It is easier for them to be a big bully
You will be surprised to hear
What some kinds are doing at a very early age
They are exposed to different kinds of drugs
Alcohol, sex, bad rap music, and guns
So join with me and let's be good to these kids
And treat all of them with respect
And when they grow up to be men and women
They will teach their children to behave properly
These kids need Christ to be in their life
Without Him, they have no hope
And this is the reason why
They find it difficult to cope.

Rupert A. Phayme
Ocala, FL

To My Son As You Graduate

It was not that long age that
We brought you home from the hospital.

It was not that long ago that
You found the kitten and thought
That the dog pen was your jungle gym.

It was not that long ago that
You were learning to rollerblade, whistle, and fish.

It was not that long ago that
Your blanket for day care was your Sea World
Shark towel and your room was full of sea creatures.

It was not that long ago that
You went with People to People to Europe for twenty days
And came back a taller, thinner young man.

And now you are a senior and ready to graduate,
And soon this will be a part of the "It was not that long ago."

Marjorie E. McClain
Pennsauken, NJ

Memories

The walls echo with sounds from the present and the past,
The empty rooms sound hollow when people speak.
Floorboards creak without the rugs on them.
Everything in the house is gone, either removed, discarded, or sold.
Dust motes float in the air. The last of the sunset, filtering through
bare windows throws a reddish cast over the dust motes.
I never thought of them as being "pretty" before this.
Everyone has left and I'm alone. This is hard,
seeing the house empty this way, knowing Mom and Dad are also gone.

Smiling, I remember the sound of my son's giggles
(he was two years old),
as he sat on grandfather's lap, being tickled.
I still hear my daughter, age fifteen,
as she did her new cheer for her grandmother.
Time has passed so quickly; both children now married,
each with three children of their own, children who will never know
what they missed by not knowing their great-grandparents.
Oh, yes, this house still holds all the happy, sad, and exciting
memories we all had as children, but they will fade
as the new owners take over and begin to create their own memories.

Eloise T. Bartosh
Scranton, PA

Angel Poem

If an angel came down from Heaven above
Would she still say that there could be love?
I see the hope in eyes that could shine
Pain is what makes them look so unkind
Loss of a loved one can make us seem blind
To the joys around us that we cannot find
Can we open our minds and our hearts in time?
Can we see the magic in people who are kind?
Kindred spirit can help you find joy
If you live through the pain you will once again
See a world where magic just never ends
It is not easy and life is unfair
The angel just asks you to please be aware
Life is too short and comes with some pain
You need to know your life is not in vain
Give to yourself
Give to your loves
Look to the sky
You will see the doves
Peace is around you if you just seek
The lesson is hard and is not for the meek
The angel is sorry you have to go through
The pain and the anguish showing on you
Tomorrow will come and she does guarantee
If you give God a chance you will soon see.

Laurie Jakeman
Smithfield, RI

Echoes . . .

from the past cried their warnings
but I didn't listen
Instead I chose to let you walk
back into my life and into my heart
Since we've become more than just friends
my hands shake when I look into
your eyes, when I see them glisten
The past has come back to haunt me
just as I knew it would
I never should have let you back in
Because of the signs I chose to ignore
I'm right back in the place I've been before
I've tried to deny your power over me
Doing everything to make you happy
I've laughed with you and cried with you
Echoes of pain are within me

Sylvia R. Green
Little Rock, AR

I was born and raised in Little Rock, Arkansas. Writing poetry has always felt a part of me. It's an expression of expression. My poem arose out of a deep internal pain of a place in my life where I was struggling. It is the personification of that place, but after conducting an exhaustive search of my mind, as the head of my own exploratory committee, I have concluded the following, I am "Sylrious".

Waiting for the Light

The sun broke through the pouring rain.
It landed on me, a yellow stain.
Grey, grey, grey is the sky.
A crack of lightning, long and bright.
Go away, clouds, just break and leave
So the flowers will come and sit with me.
The willows moved with the blades of grass.
The thunder roared, the lightning crashed.
Then came the wind blowing the leaves.
Look at them dance their dancing for me.
Another day that the sun never came.
I'll be back tomorrow to try again.

Anthony R. Davis II
Waukegan, IL

Truth

Truth is a high, mighty, noble ideal to maintain.
Deliberate truth and honesty fortifies accomplishments you gain.
Sureness of law should undoubtedly be one of your goals.
Truth will make and aid marriage
As vows ring the bells to strengthen souls.
A parable or poem may contain some deep, logical truth.
You should receive the benefits of such, beginning with youth.
So in summary, now be truthful while being your best.
Justice shall come your way, proclaiming you above the rest.

William L. Good
East Aurora, NY

The Word Is God

If you care about your future
And you really, really care
Don't let your mind
And mouth defeat you
If you really, really care
If you're poor
You named and claimed it
If you're rich
You sowed the seed
Don't go blaming other people
Look within to find the cause
Don't let it hold you in its grasp
Nor make stops 'bout your cash
What you say is what has claimed you
'Cause the Word alone is God

Inella Redmond
Baltimore, MD

A House Is Not a Home

A house can be a mansion large
Or a cabin small
Persian rugs upon the floor
Painting on the walls

Chandeliers, crystal things
Silver and much gold
But without love inside its walls
It's barren, dark, and cold

A home is just a house
Where love and joy abide
The children have respect and obey
Mom and Dad walk by their side

The children have a time for chores
And a time to play
A time to read the Bible
And with their family pray

A home is a very special place
Filled with happiness and love
And when He's made a part of it
It's blessed by God above

Jerolene D. Graves
Jacksonville, FL

215

Love, Commitment, and Motherhood

Love is feelings within the heart
Love is precious from the start
Love is giving and sharing
Love is a way of always caring

Commitment is holding on to special feelings
Commitment is also very appealing
Commitment is something very strong
Commitment is doing things right and not wrong

Motherhood is great in every way
Something new turns up every day
Motherhood is given to us by God
Motherhood is life beginning with a new part.

Mildred R. Bowman
Prince George, VA

Punalu'u Beach Park

I've lived on the Big Island since 1985
Tourists know more about this island than I
My breath was simply taken away just by the sight
To see black sand, tall coconut trees and turtles made it right
Punalu'u, you just look so awesome and so serene
I thought I went to sleep and had a beautiful dream
It's hard to realize all the hardships we face
When you see such a tranquil and enchanted place
To hear the ocean with all its melodic sounds
The sight of the black sand covering all the grounds
Countless coconut trees swaying from side to side
All the tourists' cameras flashing before the turtles take a dive
I'm sitting across from the bay on the cement blocks
Watching as the buses come down and the tourists flock
Tour bus after tour bus brings down all the people
Just so they can walk on the beach and see all the turtles
There are signs telling everyone to stay back so many feet
But in all the awe and excitement, that's a hard feat
When the crowd of people have gone and the beach is clear
You can see the turtles one by one reappear
I will hold this tranquil place dear in my heart
In the hope that maybe someday I can return to this park.

Alberta J. Rivera
Pahoa, HI

217

I, Too, Have a Dream

I have a dream, a dream deeply rooted in a Filipino
dream for a better tomorrow.
I came into this country to continue that dream,
for only in America that impossible dream is a reality.
I have a dream that one day my students will live in this
nation where they will not be judged by their home language.
but by the content of their character.
I have a dream that my students, while learning to speak
good English, won't forget their home language,
for in the words of the Philippine national hero,
Dr. Jose Protasio Rizal, "And hindi marunong magmahal sa sareling
wika ay diag pa ang hayop at malansang isda." ("Anyone who does
not love one's own language is worse than animal and odorous fish.")
I have a dream that my students will learn to respect another's
rights, for in the words of Mexico's former President,
Benito Juarez: "El respeto al derecho ajeno es la paz."
("The respect of another's right is peace.")
I have a dream that one day, my students will proud of their
national origin and their knowledge of two languages
and that they will be part of their contribution
to the county where they are now.
Then I can look back and say I was part of their success.
With this in mind, I will work harder and understand them better.
This will be the day when, with all America's children,
they will be able to say, "We speak the same language
and have the same culture."
So let their voices be heard, for in the words
of former U.S. President John F. Kennedy, "Children are
the world's most valuable resource and its best hope for the future."

Virginia Obcena Domingo
Fairfield, CA

Forgetful

Forget you like you forgot me.
What I thought was an amazing time
turns out to be a painful memory.
Please tell me what I did wrong,
I take all of the blame.
You turned out to be like all the others, the exact same.
I should've known something was wrong,
but I was blind-sighted, wrapped around your finger.
As you spoke, your lies would linger.
Take two steps forward as you push me back five.
Now I am learning that I don't need you,
you're the past, a distant memory.
I'm fine without you, this now I see,
forget you like you forgot me.

Emily A. Crook
Leetonia, OH

My Last Breath in Time

This wretched life is upon me.
in my dying hour, I cry out from the wilderness,
Is there no one to take this sorrow from me,
For I am driven to my knees.

Another faded hour has left me
Closer than the breath I took. You were
Here in my arms. You live,
For I am the life you reveled in.

I am like an unmarked grave,
Generations walked over me.
But alas, no one knows I'm here,
For I am driven to my knees.

Another faded hour has left me.
Am I not like the poor and needy
Who will always be here?
My eyes are covered by this veil of tears.
This very night, my life will be demanded from me.

But hear this,
I will perish apart from you.

My last breath in time has come forth from my lips.
My last sigh in time has gone past me.
Only for you did I live,
Now my final faded hour has left me.

Cynthia L. Randolph
Bronx, NY

I Want to Live

I want to live to help someone in life.
I don't want to be selfish or lazy,
not doing what is right.
Life is so precious,
no words can find to tell
how each part of our bodies
precisely works so well.
Our wonderful heart,
no bigger than our fist,
yet works so efficiently
and does not miss,
to pump the blood
into each delicate part.
That's our wonderful,
magnificent heart.
I want to live.

Barbara Ann Bady
Wyncote, PA

My name is Barbara Ann Bady. I was born June 9, 1931. My husband, Willie Bady
Sr., and I raised nine children. I started writing poetry after my seventh child was
born. I was inspired to write "I Want to Live" when my husband was sick after an
amputee operation. He had to take his medicine every four hours. It was 2:00 a.m.,
so I stayed awake until 4:00 a.m. I took a pad and pen on the table next to my bed.
I looked over at my husband sleeping. The thought came to my mind—I want to
live to help him.

A Love Letter

Years have passed—those moments gone
You have been away for far too long
My heart was broken that very day
When you said goodbye and went away

Memories race by, I've shed many tears
You are so far away, yet seem so near
The dreams we had all went astray
They have lived in my heart until this day

I've decided to tell you to let you know
I know there were reasons you had to go
In spite of the pain I've had to bear
I still love you—I still care

If you, perhaps, have a memory of me
I've bared my soul for you to see
Love leaves its mark—it does not fade with time
I will always love you and wish you were mine

JoAnn McBroom
Oklahoma City, OK

I Knew You When

I knew you when
You were born,
A smile upon your face.

I knew you when
You first stood,
Holding onto the chair.

I knew you when
We played ball,
Running in the front yard.

I knew you when
Your black belt
Was tied around your waist.

I knew you when
Your anger
Broke your mother's sad heart.

I know you now,
Almost grown.
You'll always be my son.

Deborah L. Andrews
Richmond Hill, GA

I am a nurse and a mom, thus spending most of my life caring for others. Now that my oldest son is leaving the nest, I was inspired to write a poem reflecting on special times in his life. My belief is that my son is destined for greatness in whatever path he takes in life. Greatness to me is not having lots of money or many things, but giving up yourself for others. Although I have made mistakes, I always tried to give up those things that I wanted for others if it was necessary. One of the people I admire the most is Mother Theresa, who said, "At the end of life, we will not be judged by how many diplomas we have received, how much money we have made, how many great things we have done. We will be judged by, 'I was hungry and you gave me to eat; I was naked and you clothed me; I was homeless and you took me in.'"

Justin

What I wish for you Justin
Reach for the stars
I know you can go far
Dream the impossible dream
Make it a reality
Never say I can't
It's always I can
I will succeed
I believe in all
I say or do
Never give up or in
I have the strength
And will prevail
Walk with your head high
Be strong and proud
Of who you are
And what you're about to become
I see great things for
You young man
Always have that
Thirst for knowledge

Mary Joe Goncalves
New Britain, CT

A Perfect Day

The skies are of a hazy blue,
The grass is streaked with silver dew.
The rays of midday sun are bright.
I see and eagle on its flight
As it wings upward out of sight.
The farmers all are sowing grain,
For soon they think that it will rain,
The brook is murmuring sweet and low.
The perfume from the flowers blows.
The singing birds fly high and low.
And now the sun sinks in the west.
A robin nests down to rest,
For now the day is almost through,
For now the darkness steals the view.
The moon is up, the stars now blink.
The shining beauties seem to wink.
The perfect day has taken flight.
To take its place, a perfect night.

Sannie M. Dennard
Morrow, GA

Toys

In the attic old dusty toys you see
Each with precious memories to be
An old worn bear a new friend you had
With him at your side you were never sad
A ball's faded color pale in sight
Many hours of fun day and night
Musical guitar's notes faint in sound
When new it blasted the entire town
A farm set you played with for hours each day
New adventures daily your own special way
A little doll with eyes so bright
Tight in your arms a friend in the night
Stacks of story books each one you knew
Read over daily enjoyment for you
Log cabin blocks many buildings you see
From towns to forts imagination to be
A bat and ball lots of wear they do hold
Many games played adventures told
Cherished moments daily of toys known
For the love of a child forever shown

Joseph H. Robert
Evansville, IL

You Are Like a Beautiful Rose

You are as delicate as a petal of a rose,
not even an petal should be harmed.
Your eyes are sparkling as the morning
dew on the grass.
Your complexion is as fair, as fair can be.
Your lips are as red as strawberry wine,
your hair flowing in the cooling
of the summer night breeze.
Like a big beautiful red
rose growing in the rose garden,
for everyone passing by to see
how beautiful you are,
not even a petal of you should be harmed.
The beauty of you makes people
happy and enjoy your beauty.
Your beauty should last a lifetime,
but it cannot; everyone knows that.
You will die away, and come back next
summer, like you always do.

Shirley A. Muir
Canyon Country, CA

I came from a small town in Nipked, Maryland. I also came from a big family of nine children. I am the youngest. When I was about fourteen years old, I would write songs. I love writing poems. I'd like to see how far I can go.

One More Day

Only in the eyes of the elderly
Do you see time that weathered the storm
As the lines on their face tell a story
Of the reflection of when they were born.
From the moment the first breath is taken
Wonderment for life begins
The journey of experience, a constant battle
A fight through the years we challenge to win.
Hoping to learn to forgive others
As well as forgive oneself
Don't carry around things that are a burden
Give a shot at striving for good health.
As age sets in and a comfort zone is reached
To sit back and enjoy a glass of lemonade
To reminisce the past memories
Hard work accomplished, weekend gatherings played.
Photos take each day back, all the treasures of time
Pulled out with the gentlest of care
Putting them back, tied with ribbons
As carefully as we dare.
Love yourself in this challenge we call life
Do smell the flowers along the way
Reward yourself for the good deeds you've done
And be ever thankful that we all get one more day.

Eileen M. Gjerde
Minden, W

Writing came to me inspired by my mother, the sweetest angel anyone could ever have the chance to meet. Listening to her wonderful words put on a page, drawing you into a story of heartfelt warmth; I was fortunate enough to have just a bit of this handed down to me. So every now and again, I have a thought of my own screaming for a pencil and paper to have the opportunity to take shape as a story or a poem, so my imagination can travel on its journey to a place from within my own soul.

J.J. the Whale

I am an orphan abandoned at sea.
Fortunately for me,
I was saved from the rough old sea.
People were kind to me.
Children cherished my
Presence in the "big hold."
When I grew to be a year old,
It was decided that I
Should learn to be bold.
I was shipped back to
The rough old sea,
Where I became just me.

Nathalie Luboff
Los Angeles, CA

A New Day

A new day, which you have not seen
Not knowing what situations or circumstances it may bring
Today of yesterday is already gone
Leaving things with the uncertain in its past that went terribly wrong
Embracing this new day as it arrives with inspirational praises,
Thanking God you're still alive
Go through this day living as if it's your last,
'Cause memories of this new day too
Will soon be part of your life's past

Cassandra R. Williams-Sykes
Memphis, TN

Love

Love invites the crucified
To experience its realm
Like a ship amidst a sea of doubt
With Jesus at the helm
Sail on to ports of peace and joy
Where pain's evaporated
To dance upon the shores of life
As Christ has intimated
But if we must traverse again
The oceans of despair
I know we're not alone, Yahweh
I've sensed Your presence there
Guide us through these times of trial
And set our spirits free
So we can love each other now
And You eternally

Stephen J. Ryan
Boston, MA

diagnosis total

you can open up your eyes now,
because you are standing beside a near-sighted son-of-a-.
you can do that leap of faith thing pretty good,
like a fresh taste of sucking
cold running water.
i can see you feel the situation.
you can also dominate a silly pleasure zone.
it can be a real turning point of temptation.
when you become a true liar.
the accent of common beauty is upon you,
with hysterical blind ambition for raising cain.
hopefully, we all can see the truth
in another political erection.
but our salvation remains to run scared,
especially
on the pumpkin eaters of humanity.
everyone has a little repressed radio of love
inside of them to be validated.
its really a probable cause for living
with a web of wicked unequivocal bright eyes.
so if your chance at heaven is breaking free,
then do it this time
with your eyes closed.

Garrison L. Moreland
Bronx, NY

If . . .

You will not cut your finger
if you don't have a knife.
Your wife won't flee for a swinger
if you don't have a wife.

If you don't have a house,
it won't be burnt or robbed.
You'll never see a mouse
if your cat does its job.

If you do not have money,
you will not fear its loss.
Your boss won't call you "Honey"
if you don't have a boss.

When you're afraid to listen,
your death's dancing nearby.
Imagine you're not existent,
and certainly you'll never die.

If sometimes God walked out,
not saying what to preserve,
think about, decide about
to have or just not to have.

Zinovy Korovin
Wharton, NJ

I emigrated to the USA from the USSR in 1979. My native language is Russian.
English is my second language. I have a wife, one son, and two stepsons. A hundred
of my Russian language poems are published by U.S. and Russian magazines and
anthologies. I'm a first prize winner in a number of my native language contests.
I'm vice-president of a New York poetry club for Russian-speaking poets. As
an English language poet, I'm an amateur. My poems in English are published
by *Poems of the World* magazine (Palatine, Illinois), *Sons of Honor* book (New
York, London, England, Paris, France) and *The International Who's Who in Poetry*
(Owings Mills, Maryland).

Safe Haven

A willow sentinel, old, proud and strong
guards the entrance to a beloved house.
The white-peaked mountains surround the yard,
while the open archer begins judging
each person that crosses his barrier.
The stoned walkway sings a story
of the family that lives beyond its post.
The random clatter inside announces
admittance is by invitation only.
Smoke emerging from the roof
is a beacon to all passersby.
This is a safe haven.
One day, I will take charge
of the sentinel, mountains, and archer,
and my story will be sung from the walkway.

Kimberly J. Acker
St. George, UT

Cans and Bottles

Cans and bottles everywhere, and what a mess they make.
Did you know that there is value in them?
How can that be?
There is something known as recycle,
Try it and you will see.
I gathered some up and took them in.
How surprised I was when I turned them in.
The paymaster said, "Sign you name here,"
Then handed me some dollar bills.
With a smile he said,
"You've earned fifty-six dollars and twenty-five cents
Because you brought in cans and bottles."
It's not just about your personal gain
When joining the recycle band,
You are really helping to protect our land.
I was delighted just knowing
I had done something to help the environment
And earned a few dollars for picking up trash.
Recycling is the thing to do.
It not only helps to preserve our land,
But gives extra money to me and you.

Bernelle Lottimore Williams
Santa Barbara, CA

Diary of Regret

All of my life, you sacrificed
You were there for each big step
You were the one who didn't let me quit
Even after all the bad things I did
Through all the mean words that I said
You still rose above, because of your love
You were my friend and companion
The one I took for granted
You always forgive, but I'll never forget
So here is my diary of regret

Kristy L. Matthews
Glen Burnie, MD

I'm a twenty-one-year-old school bus driver, and writing has always been my passion. My family has always inspired me, and it was my Aunt Sis that is the story behind my poem. She's always been there ever since I was little, and she raised me when my mother died. This poem is about the things she's done for me and the way I treated her and the regret I have for it.

Like Them That Have Gone Before

I like books.
The smell of old pages.
The texture of ink on paper.
How the binding becomes softer, opens easier to the best page.
The corners get bent.
Notes scribbled in the margin.
Lined up all along my shelves.
Just really like books.
I don't get lost on the 'Net.
I get lost in the library.
Rows and rows of stacks.
Titles on hardbacks as far as the light will reflect.
Reading words off the computer screen feels like having a pet snake.
No snuggle down and hold time.
No warm touch.
There are no mysteriously underlined passages on the screen.
No thoughts written by the person who owned it before you.
There is no history.
I want to be a person behind my time.
A living dinosaur.
A symbol of slowdom.
Like them that have gone before.
I will have my books.
I will read my books.

Leslie A. Kramer
Fort Worth, TX

My Special Angel

This lady who was my nurse truly had to be
one of God's angels sent from Heaven up above,
and as she reached out her hand to me,
her eyes were filled with truest love.
She quietly told me not to worry,
that everything would be all right.
She gave me so much strength that I needed
to make it through the longest night,
for those were all the lonely hours
that I must face that never seemed to end.
Yes, in my fretful, painful moments,
this angel was so needed, my truest friend.
She brightened up my day for me,
surrounding me with sunshine's golden light.
A quiet reverence followed her
whenever she came into my sight.
Her faith in God, she lived with every day
as she passed it on to everyone she met,
and through all my many years of life,
this truest angel, I never will forget.
This loving, giving soul, whenever she may be,
with the beating of my heart, I surely know
she is helping someone somewhere
who is in need of that special faith, the truest love,
that angel glow.

Berniece G. Piercy
Akron, OH

Nature of Life

Humans the mystery of creation, existence of life.
Beginning of creativity to explore the world where we are.
Greed and jealousy is the human heart,
made this world squander it's hard to understand.
The gloomy outcome of mistakes amid the sorrows and pain;
the imperfection of mind.
Agony we have that we are lost from compassion of universal love.
Peace broken apart, hatred and war prevails
that ruin the dignity, the value of human lives.
People departed from the rules Divinity bestowed upon us.
The only answer to achieve peace and harmony
to our descendant, that we should understand
the meaning of true life, regardless of religion,
and ideology to our tradition.
Then we can fulfill the reality of
dreams to our birth right, in the pursuit
of happiness with freedom ,the destiny of sacred life.
Humanity, the greatest tool to create the universal splendor
of faith and compassion, sacrifice and love.

Rogelio P. Purganan
Seattle, WA

There Is Always Hope

When your world is looking
Dreary and everything
Seems so wrong,
Think of all the Earth's
Beauty and then think
Of a happy song.
Because your problems
May feel like they'll
Never end
But others may have
Greater problems—
To them, your love send,
And just when you
Think happiness is no longer there,
Tomorrow will come
With hope and perhaps not a care.
So put your hope in God
And know things will work out,
For His or Her love is forever.
In your heart, this you can shout!

Lily Verhaeg
Florissant, MO

Untitled

Lord, show me a path,
a way out of this night.
My heart lives in darkness,
a soul now barren of light.

I trip through this world
like one newly blind.
My eyes blank and confused
by what it is I must find.

Lord, reach out Your hand
to one of Your weak.
My body grows weary,
a spirit humbled and meek.

I search through the blackness
as if for a flame,
my ears straining to hear
Your voice calling my name.

Lord, send me a sign,
that there's an end to this pain.
My mind echoes with chaos,
how I long to feel sane.

I pledge You life
as one who is dying.
My arms open wide,
a lost child crying.

V. Jane Benton
Lakewood, WA

Meandrous

Your anointed words fill the air with sweet perfume.
The flowers strain from their earthen homes
to drink in Your presence.
The world is Your throne and I, oh, Lord, am Your footstool.
I long to serve You, my Master, whose kind eyes beckon me home.
Down the winding path, where I so often lose my way, I pause;
"Be still," You say through the trees,
"and listen to the sound of the universe."
"They are calling your name, in a whisper, child,
they call your name."
The mist begins to clear and ever so slightly,
I see the flickering light.
You are home, waiting for me! I quicken my pace,
but a faint sound turns me around to find
that You are behind me, as well as before me.
You take my tiny hand and together we walk
to the flickering light, one soul, one dream shared by two,
unlikely warriors both taken home by Teshuva Road.

Joan V. Wiley
Goshen, NY

Daddy

Why did it take me so long to see
it was her you always wanted, it was never really me.
I guess that explains why she gets all your attention and love.
She's the one you are always proud of,
never me.
Seems like I'm always the problem,
always me.
Guess it will always be her that gets put first,
never me.
It's okay, Daddy, I know now why you left.
It was her you always wanted, it was never really me.
But it's okay because one day, I will come first.
Yes, me.
There's someone that is proud of me.
Yes, me.
She understands because you did it to her too.
You left her along with me.
Yes, me.
She's always been there when you just couldn't be.
She will always be there for me when I need her.
Yes, me.

Catherine N. Ankerich
Hartwell, GA

What a Woman

She stands tall with confidence large in heart.
She's proud of herself in any direction she walk.
What a woman!

Her skin smooth, brown, and chocolate.
Her voice soft, smooth, and yet so sharp,
It can win any man's heart.
What a woman!

As she enters into a room, you will know,
For this Black woman will take the floor.

With her hips swaying from side to side,
You'll clearly see she has nothing to hide.

Strutting her stuff with all she has,
This Black woman is one bad ass.
What a woman!

Charlotte E. Mosley
Stone Mountain, GA

I would like to say we as women of color must know and understand who we are, realize who we are, and last but not least, walk with confidence. Respectfully and with standards.

On the Wharf

The great beauty seized my soul; ships
Swinging as grand geese all time, continue
To flaunt daytime in the night, hurl into
Water stream their weighty anchors deep.

Seagulls' shouts hanged in the head-wind,
Clouds' wrinkles were smoothed out. North's the
Strong wind haggled with west, south, east.
This wind snuggled up to the ships' wharf, where

Sadly, the tight rope creaked as door.
Fascinated waves gazed on the sunset,
Restless water has quelled noises, clunks and
Splashes of the ship's screw near the wharf.

Amorous pair goes down to the shore
Over the short gangplank, licked by indiscreet
Envious waves rustling all more, "con amore."
There is amorous pair, waves, a quay, the street.

Felix Reinstein
Brooklyn, NY

Memories of Mom

Her memories will remain with us
as long as Christians dwell upon the Earth.
You know, moms have a special place in our lives;
we learn her voice ad touch from the time of conception.
Their is no doubt we caused a bit of discomfort
before we took our first breath of air,
but her awesome love remained with us everywhere.
Mother didn't die, she just moved to another place.
Her new home is a mansion, where her family will join her one day.
You can communicate with her by air mail,
the new address is The House of God
on Heavenly Boulevard Zip Code 3534-n856
(eternity) in care of Jesus Christ.
This mansion has millions of private lines
if you would like to give her a call.
Her new number is very simple;
all you need to do is pray aloud.
I'm sure she will recognize your voice
and enjoy whatever you have to say.
There is no doubt she will be peering down on you
and sending wisdom to guide your day.

Donald L. Claflin
Beaver Dams, NY

I have been writing for about fourteen years. I write mostly spiritual poetry and
verse. I started writing shortly after having my fourth back operation. It left me
disabled. My collection of poetry is at seven hundred, ninety titles.

The Viewing Is Free

Beneath my feet a carpet of green
How blue the roof over my head
God's treasures all sandwiched in between
Of Queen Anne's lave and roses red.

Chasing a firefly all around
Catching and placing in a jar
Some flying high, some low to the ground
Watching them light up like an evening star.

Listening to the mighty ocean's roar
Each wave coming and going at their own pace
Deposits of shells left on sandy shores
Wondering how far they have come in their race.

Over the mountains, the moon brightly shines
Comes the lonely call of the whippoorwill
Shadows of gray from swaying pines
Sweet smell of blossoms lingers still.

God paints a picture most everywhere
We have only to open our eyes to see
Of meadows, valleys, brooks are all there
Painted for the viewing and the viewing is free.

Nancy Marie Grant
Taylorsville, NC

Gentle Death

I'm unwanted and unkept
My eyes alone show I've wept
A second chance should fate allow
Dreamless slumber is best for now
Taken in your hands of care
My need no longer to beware
Silent tears you shed for me
No pain I feel. . . . At last I'm free.

Tracey L. Garrett
Wichita, KS

Wondering Why

Have you ever been so lost you feel
life is not worth the extra zeal?
Remember your darkest day seemed so long
and time stood still and then it was gone?
It took your breath away and you had to say,
if it weren't for my faith, I'd fade away.
Then out of the blue came the will to keep on,
and I'm not quite sure if I can go beyond.
Wondering why I am always afraid of trying,
and this gift is so sure, it leaves me crying.
Yes, I will try one more time.
I ask why,
because there will be no more wondering why.

Gale A. Ciampi
Auburn, NY

Beneath Your Wing

When no moon in height, no clouds
When stars feel lonely in the evening sky
Then come to me, my dear little swan
From fairy tale.
Please, come.

Beneath your wing, I'll clean my own feather
I'll dress myself in pristine crystal white
Completely different from whom I still remember
Completely different
The woman I've become.

My grown soul has so many faces
God knows I have changed them many times
I was a string, a violin, an orchestra . . .
So many played on me
And I have played sometimes.

My whole life I hoped for somebody
To share thoughts, to love, to cheer me up
A single note can't produce a melody
Your silent presence
Never was enough.

Beneath your wing, I'll clean my own feather
Until my mission will be fully done
I'm so different from whom I still remember
I'm so different,
My dear little swan.

Tatiana S. Podgoretskaya
Vienna, VA

The Sheep, the Shepherds—a Parable

We are on the hillside, we are all wet and cold
The storm has come upon us, the storm has split the fold
Our shepherds are not with us, they have gone somewhere to pray
We sheep have lost direction; please Lord, be with us today
We have lost our shelter, we have lost our way
Some have gathered together, some have gone away
We are all frightened; what now do we do?
We need our shepherds to teach us and learn to follow You
We hear someone approaching, we hear them as they call
We are not alone now, not alone after all
There on the hillside, the footsteps are so clear
The footsteps of my shepherd are finally coming near
But we hear two voices, one near, one far away
The shepherds have agreed to work together,
And have answered our prayer today
The sheep say, "Thank You, Lord, for what You have done today"
The shepherds shake hands, give a hug, and then kneel down to pray
The fold is now growing, new sheep every day
God smiles down, the twenty-third psalm
For the sheep gave the sermon today!

Ellen K. Webb
Monticello, IL

Chain of Operations

Each is like a link and when a link goes away,
A space, a gap is present.
Most of us work around it, most of us don't notice it.
But on a rarity, a few of us will take notice of the gap,
The emptiness of the lonely, possibly forgotten link
To the human chain of operations.
Seeking, finding the forever tugging question,
How do we best find peace?

Deborah L. Elliott
Belleville, MI

Heartache

Fire and ice is what we've become.
The past years have changed us.
Love may no longer be enough.
Our hearts and souls are no longer one,
And the pain of it all has just begun.
They say that time, it heals all wounds,
So why can't my heart find the way on its own?
It hurts every day, the pain is intense.
I don't know the way, nothing makes any sense!
So why do I sit here day after day
Hoping to awake and finally find my way?
It hurts way too much to continue on.
I hope that someday, the heartache will be gone.

Chris Ann Aubuchon
Hardwick, VT

She

She lays in the dark
Wondering what went wrong
Her heart breaking
Listening to their song

As day breaks
And the sun shines
She puts on her face of all being fine
She moves through the world one step at a time
Wondering if she will ever be free
Of the ache in her heart she thought would never be

The day ends
The sun sets low
The moon rises to a beautiful glow

Another night she lays in the dark
Wondering what went wrong
Her heart breaking
Listening to their song

Cindy L. Bojorquez
Gilbert, AZ

The Sun Will Shine

You wish the clouds would roll away,
but the dark clouds came back today.
You said you don't know what to do,
in the cloud you feel like your world has fallen too.
The sun will shine one day, you'll see,
there will be peace of mind for your family.
You see people in the street, nowhere to sleep,
kids with no clothes or shoes on their feet.
Mom's been abused, beaten to a puff,
fathers getting killed trying to sell that stuff.
Keep on going, don't give up,
even though your life might seem rough.
You'll see the sun peeping through the cloud,
it will make you run, and sing out loud.
No matter how bad your day gets,
don't run to the drug man for that fix.
Fall to your knees, and say a little prayer,
you can count on God, he's always there.
You'll see one day, the sun will shine,
all you have to do is keep this in mind.

Mary M. Thompson
Richmond, VA

Pets

Pets are so very loving and truly dear
No matter what kind you choose to be near
A pet responding to your voice when heard
It may be a dog, cat, rabbit, pig, or bird
A horse, pony, mouse, rat, or a special snake
Whatever kind you choose to lovingly take
A pet that will warm your heart with cheer
Spending fun time with them through the year
There may be caring pets I did not mention
Some other types that draw your attention
Pets bring loyalty and true sharing affection
Joining our hearts with a fond connection
A dog you can take for a walk down the street
Maybe a friend or two you may also meet
A cat will come and jump on your lap
Purring and purring to take a little nap
A pony or a horse you may take for a ride
Or just rub his or her nose and walk beside
A rabbit may thump its feet and go hopping along
While a bird will be in its cage, singing a song
Other pets have their own special, personal way
Making you happy with their tune and play
All pet owners have a loyal responsibility to protect their pet
Any kind of pet deserves sincere respect and never, ever neglect

Leola E. Jackson
Gilroy, CA

Sands of Love

Love, so like sand, since the beginning of time,
So tender when scattered, it sifts through my mind.
So easy to slip away, it can't tell where it belongs,
And if whispered too loudly, in an instant it's gone,
But it always refills, with hurt in its place,
Why couldn't this exchange be like mosaic to grace?

Love, so like sand, has slipped right through my hands,
The need is so great, it's like supply and demand.
Just to have love, steep mountains I'd climb,
I'll swim great seas, I'll travel through time.
Let me emphasize for you how important it is to me,
It's like what sun is to life or even sand is to sea.

Love, so like sand, created for woman and man,
If love had ears to hear my heart, then it would understand
That wounded hearts from abandoned times
Find it very hard to mend
Until the loneliness is broken, and no more bitterness within.
When God created love, also creating woman and man,
They were intended to drift together and forever
Through marriage, vows, and band.

John W. Hagans
Dayton, OH

Arms Held Open Wide

He holds His arms wide open
With a smile on His face
As He welcomes yet another
Into His humble place.

Departing may be difficult
As we shed a tear and more
As we try to go on living
Just like we've done before.

God promises to care for them
Just like He cares for you
And when the road is rough ahead
He'll be there to get you through.

We may not understand it
And question with a why
But His arms are still wide open
As for the departed one we cry.

Leslie A. Horvath
New Paris, IN

Americans, Stand Tall

At this time of great infamy,
Dear Lord, help us to see
The way that we must go to win;
Make this our destiny.

Americans, Americans,
Stand tall! Stand tall to fight
The terror that envelops us;
Let's strive for what is right!

Lost, bewildered, we've been wronged,
Our pain will not be stilled,
For hate to us, we must show love;
Lord, help us to be strong.

Americans, Americans,
Stand tall! Stand tall to fight!
Join with other friendly nations
To rid this world of blight.

Let love's endurance conquer all,
Do not let hate creep in.
To do this task, we must stand tall!
Stand tall we must to win!

Christine Dowdall M. Schult
Sedona, AZ

December 2008

A shiny copper shield, and another
Tarnished silver over a white gold—Mars and the moon,
The god of war facing our planet's sister.
Too close, a foot or two, in the navy blue sky,
So crystal clear, embraced by the silent dance
Of the ancient constellations. The northern hemisphere.
What a spectacle over the broken heart of the Earth.
Only three nights before Christmas.
You can hear nonstop carols for peace, joy,
And voices of angels.
You lift your head to examine again the masterpiece:
A shiny copper shield, and another
Tarnished silver over a white gold.
The weather is chilly, aren't You shivering?

Rada O. Gudjoukova
Alexandria, VA

Passionate

As I sit here wondering what to do
My mind automatically thinks of you
Your smile your touch your tenderness and your warm embrace
Your face seems so far away but I still see
The little wrinkle on your cheek
I love the words you wrote to me
It was like poetry as far as I can see
The bittersweet aroma of your scent
Your passionate words made me weak in the knees
I couldn't stand I couldn't walk all I could hear
Was you telling me you love me now and forever
Holding your hand out to me as I approached the door
Calling my name with such a sweet sound
Baby this is our time around
Backing up my energy to roll to the front
Never knowing a love so pure that could make me feel you so near
Once in a lifetime you feel this kind of passion
Once in a love time you feel this reaction
Take it in stride and enjoy the moment
Hold on to this dream because it is true
That I found a love that is as passionate as you

Carol B. Hammond
Bolingbrook, IL

The Unclaimed

To one, a lover, the other, a friend.
A brand-new beginning, or an imminent end.

Conceiving a passion, or aborting a friendship.
To live with the second? I couldn't stand it.

So I grasp the needle, my mouth I've sewn shut
'Cause keeping us close wasn't just luck.

But being your friend's not what took me aback,
You know you and me can't help but attract.

It's the longing for you that I can't ever show,
I must cut off emotion so feelings won't grow.

But when something is severed, it just grows back longer,
The heart cries out louder, the passion much stronger.

So I hold back tears that can never be known,
And the longer I do, my eyes overflow.

But this longing I hold can't see light of day,
So here's to the love I can't ever claim.

Rachael C. Cook
Tieton, WA

After the Storm

As I sit here looking out my window today,
The sun's not shining, and the clouds are gray.
Looks like a storm is brewing in the west.
The animals scurrying, and Mother Robin in her nest.
The trees are swaying, and the wind is starting to blow.
It's lightning and thundering and putting on a real good show!
The rains are coming, you can hear the sound
Of happy raindrops falling to the ground,
And if you can look past all those showers,
You'll be able to see some of the most beautiful flowers!

Cindy L. Grubbs
Ashland, OH

Joyful Creations

One tiny patch of blue peeks out of the gray sky,
Yet God in all His glory put this beauty in our eye.
Soon the clouds will part, sunshine will abound.
In this crisp, new spring, we hear a different sound.
Listen, hear them coming, the flowers from the earth.
Everything moved as God creates rebirth.
Beautiful now the colors, snappy is the air.
Tiny creatures dance, having not a single care.
Warmth now surrounds them, snow is long gone.
Joy, so wonderful like the coming of the dawn.
We thank You for the coming of the spring.
With a joyful heart, creation's praises we now sing.

Lola F. Moore
Spokane, WA

The Deckhand

He rises before the morning sun
to prepare for the dawning day
A lot of work there is to be done
before the ship may sail away

The air is clean and brisk
as if filtered by the night
The vapors from his breath
condense in the early light

He greets the fog in a kindly way
as if they were old friends
whistling along the dock of the bay
to the boat in which he tends

The vessel is still and gray
he shall bring it back to life
The deckhand will care for her every day
much the same as a man for his wife

The captain arrives at the port slip
and the crew sets sail away
but the deckhand will be the one tending the ship
when the rest go home for the day

Scott C. Sheldon
Garibaldi, OR

You Believe

As I have sat here
and thought about my life
a lot of things missing
and not knowing what is right
Listen to what I've been told
or told not to listen at all
Not knowing what's been right
or what's real at all
My world has been confused
turning in all different ways
not knowing what I'm looking for
or that special person who could say
Too many things I've lost
most of my life a glare
I can taste it on the tip of my tongue
but within minutes it's not there
Feeling trapped in my own mind
it's not a pretty sight to see
and all you can do is step back
'cause you're the one who believes

Catherine A. Taylor
Lafayette, IN

In 1992, I had an aneurysm rupture in my brain. I was in a coma, and when I woke up, I had lost eighteen years of my life. I did not know I was a mother of three grown children. I was starting over, relying on what family and friends told me as to what my life had been before. Many times what was told to me by friends was completely different than what was told to me by family. This poem comes from years of trying to find myself and the true friendship of one person who believes in me, no matter what my past holds.

For You Make Me

For you make me feel like I can
be natural around you, like the
naturalness of water flowing through
the river, at ease like the stillness
of the lake.

For you make me feel like smiling to
no end, 'cause in my heart I know
it ain't pretend.

For you make me feel good like
prayer to the soul.
For you make me feel like asking, oh, God,
have I found my pot of gold?

For you make me feel happy like
the story of a ring to no end.
For you make me.

Iris M. Rios
Boardman, OH

Roseanna

Whenever I think of you,
I must catch my breath.
My heart skips a beat,
and I begin to sweat.
It isn't merely an anxiety attack,
but a full-blown Roseanna seizure.

Just as the waves upon the shore
keep on coming back for more,
a small taste of you
makes me cry more, more, more!
What was once desire from a distance
suddenly is necessary for my existence.
You capture all my thoughts and I am obsessed
with our next caress.
What is this power that you hold over me
that captures all my energies
and pulls them to your breast
and leaves me imagining
you and I enmeshed
in an embrace,
together, forever.

Stanley Zielinski
Lexington, KY

This Entourage of Bewilderment

The heart, 'tis the ultimate center sphere of influence,
How it holds the feelings of nostalgia,
Memories, sweet and tender, kind and loving,
Rapport that elates the heart to sing,
Of all the sentimental yearning,
Of wishing wells of hope and dreams.

Deep within it holds the cravings and the substances
Of all existence, as when its sad,
It beats as if to die,
It feels crushed, brokenhearted, in deep anguish.
When excited, it beats like a drum jubilantly intent,
As the drum-master, at the head, leading the parade,
Announcing and making a statement of joy and content.

This entourage of bewilderment and contentment,
Though at times of overwhelming proportion,
Contrite aspects of hurts, pain, news of misfortune,
But as well as good, elation arises expectations,
If righteous and fine in this world of prognostication.

As assuring fortune of ecstasy probes the heart,
Of all its profound mysteries and all that it holds,
As spheres of beauty, symmetry of splendors,
Make my heart to love life and embrace faith,
As overtures of rhapsody fill my heart to overflow,
As my heart grows stronger, I ponder on mercy and grace.

Elena V. Rivera
Tampa, FL

untitled

the little children are playing
in the parking lot again
i hear them talking and laughing

sometimes when it is too loud
i think they are talking to me
but that is not true
i just think they are

i can't seem to squeeze
their voices out of my head
when i think i start hearing them talking to me

i just don't know how
to make the talking go away

i just don't know how. . . .

Suzanne Belmont
Cincinnati, OH

From My Kitchen Window

I have such a lovely sight,
and late autumn is when it is just right
when all of our other beautiful trees
have completely lost their leaves,
and are in their winter rest,
bare and leaf undressed;
for the winter, gone is their beauty,
but still performing their duty
for one exception,
standing there all aglow,
putting on its autumn show
with its black trunk covered by
vivid red, orange, yellow, and green,
what an awesome, heartwarming scene!
Thank You, Lord, for this gorgeous sight,
I am blest with true delight.
Soon the winter winds will blow,
but now, I can enjoy from my kitchen window!

Billie A. Francis
Indianapolis, IN

Let's Go Hunting!

Some fellas love to go hunting,
They hunt for all kinds of wild game.
They think the more game they can get,
It'll bring them lots of fame.
To go hunting you need a license,
I never figured out what for.
Then one of my buddies told me why—
That knocked me to the floor!
Now I won't hesitate to tell the world,
Mom and Dad didn't raise a fool.
I learned one thing about hunting
That doesn't sound very cool.
That hunting license is so much like
Our marriage license today,
SO I'll never go hunting as long as I live,
Or at least here's why I say.
The reason I'll never go hunting is
That license fills me with fear;
I found out in the ol' USA
They both only allow you one dear!

Donald E. Murphy
Xenia, OH

Gone, but Not Forgotten

In memory of David C. Gerwolds,
my grandfather, father figure, and friend

Gone, but not forgotten, most would say.
How to live for such a stay?
Here on Earth, the world spins 'round
with such memories; keep your feet on the ground.
To be stern or somewhat steady,
party on through such confetti.
Life brings a world of wind
to hold the hand of my dear friend.
Boots on or my boots off, I'm still me,
a mother, wife, sinner, saint, too much to see.
We all at some point must realize
there is more to me than meets the eyes.
The shoes, we all at some point fill.
With your heart, there is will.
The power of our minds, bodies and souls
for such emotional control.
A life should be so simple to see
what would or will lie before me?
A path not wilted but somewhat tread,
throughout my journey, God has led.
A handshake, a proud welcome for me.
A hand-brushed painted sea.
Washed and withered away for a small fee.
Advantages all passed down to me;
without you, and I, where is then we?
Support, love, a gentle caress,
a kind poise throughout this mess.
Emotionally disturbed, a slight fight to earn such a right.
Inner peace, a soul driven spirit of release.
Gone, but not forgotten, most would say.
How to live for such a stay?
Life brings a world a wind
to hold the hand of my dear friend.

Christina M. Rowland
Ruffin, NC

269

Sands of Time

Splinter in the hourglass, the sands of time can't be restrained
As the sun sinks, burns its peace into every blade of grass
The centuries each are counted in the grains
When the wind blows across the sand
It's like watching pyramids vanish
Ten thousand years after Man—
And when the wind blows through the trees,
It's like unknown secrets whispered from eternity

All that can be realized is waiting to be defined—
Empires rise and fall, are lost beneath the drifting sands of time

Did Atlantis exist? Was Shamballa a place or a myth?
There's a sandstorm rising higher
Against the fading face of the Sphinx
The Nile River is going drier
As civilizations one by one fall extinct

Following a trail to the fall of Man,
Where money, power, and greed were the holy grail
Despite all the wealth, in poverty fell, swept away by eon's hand
Is there a way to save ourselves from the future
That the Mayans foretell?
What will be the legacy of Man long after 2012?

All that can be realized is waiting to be defined—
Empires rise and fall
Are lost beneath the drifting sands of time. . . .

Joe Doherty
Lincoln Park, MI

A Positive Mind Equals a Happy Life

Say yes, turn it all on, and

Let the game on life begin!

Recognize our powerful gold mine within us

Use Your many God-given talents

Dream your dreams

Say, "I know I can"
Building up your confidence
And inner strength
For the journey of life

Count your blessings
Throughout the day

See the good in a problem to be
turned into an opportunity

Look upwards
With blinders for negativity

Worry is the most useless of habits
For a positive mind equals a happy life

Elizabeth R. Langlois
Parksley, VA

When I was ten years old, my mother gave the family the story "The Little Engine That Could." "I think I can," she said to always live by. Well, that day, I vowed to write a classic for children to help them and live on forever. I read a library's worth of success books. In 2001, I graduated from the Institute of Children's Literature. I wrote two manuscripts with art. Later, I found I had a talent in poetry. Whenever I had a problem or an idea, I would write the title and the poem would flow from the pen. I have been honored with three outstanding achievements from the International Library of Poetry. This poem is a synopsis of my philosophy to live by.

You Can't Saw Sawdust

You can't saw sawdust,
It's already been done;
You can saw and saw and saw,
But the results will be none.

But you can squeeze lemons,
And make some lemonade.
Experience is the foremost teacher
From the mistakes we have made.

Ned E. Hoopingarner
Ellenton, FL

My dad owns a lumberyard and a millwork shop, too. He handed me a broom. I knew what to do. There is a fragrance in sawdust as it penetrates the air. I enjoy the job of sweeping. You do when you care. Sawdust is the fine leavings of a craftsman's art. Thank God for craftsmen when it comes from their heart.

Grieving

All my life, I knew you as the funny one
You would make people smile so bright
as if you were looking at the sun
and the joy you brought will never be erased
You will always be in my heart, I'll never forget your face
It hurts so much to know that you're gone
Feels like the other day
we were riding around, listening to that funny song
You know the song, the one with the crazy words
and then we went to Burger King because you loved your Whoppers
It hurt so much that I couldn't say goodbye
so I wrote this poem as my last try
Your life here may be over, but up there it starts anew
I feel a little better knowing Grandma is with you
I'll always miss you, that's never going to change
and the pain that's in my heart will always remain
but I know one day I will see you again
The time here that is lost, up there we'll get to spend
I just wanted to write this to let you know that I love you
so rest in peace, Uncle Oscar, I'll never forget you.

Dolce Lofton
Middletown, NY

Someone Special

Someone special passed away the other day
For the first time, I did not know what to say
I went to the window looking for a sign
Only to see his reflection, not mine
Seeing the snow fall in groups of nine
My mind started to reflect in time
Each flake represented a different experience in time
There were flakes of joy
There were flakes of pain
There were flakes of laughter
Even one of the thereafter
As the snow became heavy, the flakes became many
Many times to cherish his time on Earth, which became many
As the snow began to decrease
I knew this moment was about to cease
For the season was about to end
I thought about his life from the beginning to the end
I turned my head and headed for bed
I reflected on what Jesus said
Why seek the living among the dead
So I knelt before my bed
I heard a voice that said
As long as his spirit is alive in your hearts and minds
He will always live through the end of time

William W. Price
Providence, RI

When Colors Fade

When black conquers blue
And brown takes over green
The world will be sad and dreary
When orange disappears
And stars fade away
What will be here other than
Sadness
Despair
And cold?
When purple is tired
And pink grows old
So will the life once flourished
When red is extinguished
And yellow grows dim
What could possibly keep us
From falling away?
White!
Light that will never fail us
And will keep us from destruction
It is pure
And it will bring back color to our world
And all white wants in return
Is for us to be careful
And never let it happen again.

Amanda M. Schuller
Ottawa, OH

Memories

I heard a laugh the other day.
It came from just across the way.
Was it my love's? But as I turned,
The source of it had gone away.

My mind pushed back the lonely years.
My eyes then overflowed with tears
As that dear voice my heart caressed
With memories of happiness.

I saw a shadow on the snow.
It looked like his and yet I know
My heart must finally let him go. . . .
He died so many years ago.

Maria B. Meyer
Narrowsburg, NY

Civil War

Guns drawn
Swords drawn
Bayonets fixed
The order is given
To charge is ordered.

North soldiers
South soldiers
Collide into chaos
People are dying
Under each other's bayonets.

People are stabbing
People are fighting
Fighting to survive
The war.

The South retreats
The North
The Union soldiers
Have won the war.

Andrew E. Romanowski
Rockville, MD

Window to Your Soul

As I look into your eyes
I slowly slip into a better place
They are the color of a midnight sky
You always bring a smile to my face
I want to open up to you
To ask if you love me too
Your eyes are a window to your soul
But the drapes have been pulled shut
Your love is my only acquittal
I want to tell you these things, but
To this question, I know the answer
You see a friend and nothing more
To your other relationship, this is a danger
You are the one I truly adore
I'd give anything for just one chance
To show you true romance
So I'll keep these feelings inside
Behind my eyes, my love will hide
Never to see the light of day
Unfortunately, there is no other way

Elmer L. Mardis
Booneville, MS

Back from the Brink

Burdened by tragedy
Amongst the worst that could befall
Frozen in time winter's icy wrath
Without tangible purpose found
Stricken by the insurgence of grief
A stencil impressed so indelibly
As the sadness seed erupted in me
Like a hollow sounding trumpet
The fire within me all but smothered
A flame of embers burning ever so dimly
Before an echo searching to be heard
To be silenced no more
Wailing words of sorrow from an abyss
As sunlight chased my dark shadows
A wiser walk I began to take
Autumn's yellow spotted leaves
Being crushed under my footsteps
While all my thoughts swirling in my head
Consumed my fleeting spirit like an opus
A brilliant repertoire inside me
No more waiting for twilight sleep
My life now redefined
My life once again worth living

Gail F. Cushing
Massapequa, NY

Time

Looking back in a younger man
Time stood still
And it never seemed that two worlds could grow apart
It was all for one and one for all
Straight from the heart
Life on the streets has taught him
To see the world through different eyes
To think he could have it all
The world is his to take
For one to see is more than one simple look
To hide behind the light
When starry nights, when each wish
Is a vanishing star
Once for the rains that never end
Living in an age of innocence
In the shadows of a brighter day
The danger to hide
To wash away his troubles and sorrow
To fill his heart up with emptiness
Bring back those raindrops and wash his cares away
And dry his eyes with the sunlight
And on that star is one small wish

Danielle M. Boatwright
Hartsville, SC

Meant to Be

Crash, boom, all I hear
Sirens ringing in my ears
Fear us all is all I hear, face yourself in the mirror
Day by day, we're all scared
Speak with your mouth, and not just your mind
Don't speak out and another dies
Bombing for peace, oh, the money and greed
Strange how we're blind, but can still see
It's you and I causing these things
Slowly the world falls apart
Empty your trash or empty your heart
Fire a gun or a new idea
Save a child or take their freedom
Maybe after this, you still can't see
But one girl can't fix everything
Sing a song or let out a sigh
Make a difference or let the world die
It's not just up to me
You have the power, not used wisely
It's your chance because I can see
Some things just aren't meant to be

Mariah N. Dinya
Cleveland, OH

Achievement

How ready is the man of medicine.
His skills in pathology, psychiatry,
Human resources are unparalleled
In his depth to heal the unwell.
Through his genius in medical knowledge,
He stands abreast among the scholars.
This former husband of mine
Is dedicated to healing mankind,
Therefore, sweet love, may God
Bless you in all your endeavors.

Frances Watson
Rockville, MD

I am an African-American. I received a B.A. degree in sociology and psychology.
I worked on an M.B.A. three years and took five law courses, constitutional law,
administrative law, commercial law, labor law, and the legal environment of
business. I learned five languages, German, French, Spanish, Latin, and Japanese.
I was elected to Alpha Kappa Delta, the National Sociology Honor Society. I am
a member of the American Association of University Women and the Metropolitan
Opera Guild of New York City. I worked as a stenographer for the United States
Department of Justice. I was also a social science analyst for the United States
Department of Health and Human Services.

Love's Gifts

I'll give to you a magic wishing star
To make your fondest dreams come true,
The golden treasure from the rainbow's jar,
The crack'ling thunderbolt, the dawn's fresh dew.

I'll give to you a merry carousel
To bring you happiness life through,
The silv'ry music of a tinkling bell,
The warmth of home and hearth, a babe's first mew.

I'll give to you the shining silv'ry moon
To pledge my love each month anew,
The peaceful stillness of the deep lagoon,
The shelter of my arms when a storm is due.

I'll give to you a diamond wedding ring
To make you mine for all life through,
The tender rosebud in the early spring,
Deep love and tenderness, my life for you.

Simmin H. Labell
Peabody, MA

Dead Flowers

New growth, fresh and green,
straining toward the sun.
Rain softly kisses the petals as they unfurl,
growing straight and strong—
a promise of beauty.

Sun heats, rain evaporates,
petals and leaves stretch high,
absorbing the warmth, dancing in the breeze—
lush bloom, full of color.

Colors fade—leaves droop, petals fall,
stems bow toward the ground
as the wind slaps them down.
Rain ceases and the sun loses it heat,
struggling to survive—
dead flowers.

Pressed in my heart—
a remembrance.

Shelia L. Newcomb
Ellicott City, MD

I Found You

I love you
As the sun
Kisses the moon
I love you
As the day light
Set unto and on
Wondrous ways
You are love sent
To before the plan
We are linked
To be mechanisms
Meant to care
Dwell and to love
As we shall burn
For we are happy
When we are together

Paula J. Pierce-Acosta
Mt. Vernon, NY

Rest in Peace, Poppy, We Love You

I never knew this day would come,
Seeing you laying there hooked up to machines in the hospital bed.
No one could ever imagine what was going through your head.
We sat there to hold your hand,
But no one could truly understand.
We hated to see you suffer in pain.
It was just driving everyone insane.
Now that you're leaving, we feel so alone,
But everyone knows the angels are taking you home.
You will be forever missed.
It really hit me giving you that one last kiss.
Everyone's eyes built up with tears.
I could just imagine your fear.
We hate that it had to go this way.
We will miss you each and every day.
Now we just keep sitting here, saying our goodbye,
Thinking to ourselves, "Why?"
You were such a great guy.
No one will ever know why you had to die.
Our hearts are broken, as you know.
It's just too hard letting you go.

Shana M. Butler
Waterbury, CT

I Stood Upon the Hill

I stood upon the hill green valley below,
I shouted and the echoes flowed
Granny! Granny! Granny!
Make the fire glow! To Granny I go!
I stood still upon the hill
And listened as the echoes
Flowed over the valley below
Cows were grazing in the meadow
Birds were chirping, it was early morning
The forest wind blew
Trees and branches swayed, day was dawning,
Fruits were falling; hey, fella! Good morning!
I stood still upon the hill
And listened as the echoes flowed
Over the valley below
Quack, quack, shouted the ducks swimming in
The pond; this place was Long Pond
Tweet, tweet, sang the sparrow; Mary dead, who killed her?
I yelled! A dove flew in the willow
I stood still upon the hill
And listened as the echoes flowed
Over the valley below
Moo, moo bellowed the cows,
Calves sucked its mother's breast,
Skies were blue, just a few; in the valley below,
His mother was a Jew! Hey, fella!
Flowers red, white, and blue open to greet the sun,
This place was fun! Under the sun! Wow, I yelled!
I stood still upon the hill
And listened as the echoes flowed
Over the valley below

Phillis Freeman
Jamaica, NY

287

Untitled

There is but one sound,
One voice,
One word.

There is but one look,
One hug,
One kiss.

There is but one thought,
One feeling.

If only she knew

The word,
The kiss,
The feeling.

If only she cared.

Jeffrey S. Gorman
Meadville, PA

Silence

There's the silence of the night
When the children are asleep
And the quiet snow is falling,
Falling softly, white, and deep.

There's the silence of the twilight
When birds have stopped their song.
The solitude of evening
While time moves slowly along.

In the quiet of the garden,
Underneath a silvery moon
The night-blooming jasmine
Fills the air with sweet perfume.

Then a sudden gentle breeze
Cools the worries of the day.
The world will soon be dreaming
Until dawn's first bright ray

Florence F. Schnitzer
Royal Palm Beach, FL

Adirondack Trees in Winter

The hard winds have stripped the brilliant colors from the trees.
The leaves are gone and now the trees are bare.
Soon will come the blast of winter's freeze.
These are times when nature's cycle does not seem fair.

The naked trees stand silent in the winter cold,
And soon their limbs will hold the falling snow
When nature's winter story will unfold
As the naked trees will bend when the fierce wind blow.

Robert E. Graves
Ticonderoga, NY

I was born in Providence, Rhode Island in 1931. I am the only child of Henry and Florence Nightingale. I have three daughters, Karen, Susan, and Leslie. My wife passed away two years ago. I started writing poetry when I was in high school over sixty years ago. Over the past four decades, I have had many poems published and have received many awards for my poetry. During World War II, I was a choir boy at the Cathedral of St. John the Divine in New York City. In my early thirties, I had two auditions with the Metropolitan Opera and sang on television. In recent years, I sang with a wonderful choral group known as the Canterbury Choral Society, and with this group I twice sang at Carnegie Hall. I currently live in the Adirondacks, where I have seen the beauty and felt the fury of Mother Nature.

In Memory of Ben

Sometimes in my weakest hour,
A voice would talk to me,
Never give up, it says,
Stay fast and depend upon me.

I've heard this voice so often,
Sometimes I'd listen,
But most times, I did not.

This voice, so soft and gentle,
It's been my anchor many nights.
I've held on tight through all the storms.
Without it I'd be like a flag,
Beaten, battered, and worn.

This voice I hear so often
Is Jesus Christ, the Lord.

So when your world becomes disheveled,
And it seems like there's no end in sight,
Get down on your knees, and reach up to the Lord,
And He will make everything all right.

Marilyn Dian Pennington-Shifflett
Hambleton, WV

Kinetic

Velocity unmatched
out of nowhere
stopped in its tracks
skull in the mud
vitality blood
depart the low path
and ascend far above
then greet a cloud
as strife does dispel
a gust of fresh air
from which to propel
and with new perspective
unlocks new objective
nonsense deflected
by brain waves electric

Mark P. Greene
Woodbridge, VA

Storm

A heavy breeze picks up,
winds start blowing through the trees,
turning over the fresh, green leaves.

Black shrouds cover the sky,
engulfing this world that is mine.
A boisterous rumble of thunder growls through the sky,
echoing in my mind.

A flash of lightning pierces
the black sky, a downpour of
rain floods the cracked, black
pavement below the soles of my
saturated sneakers.

In this world of mine, I must
sometimes wonder if I should hurry
out from under this grey world that is mine,
for acid may one day fall from the sky

in this world that is . . .

yours
and
mine.

Kim M. Ostrowski
Yonkers, NY

Breathe within Me

My heart drifted beneath the sea,
Silencing the cry of roaring waves
That woe my existence with trembling fears.
Running to my hiding place,
My journeys seem helpless.
I lay at your resting place and asked for at least,
"Grant me your breath within me."
Breathe in me,oh, Lord and I will live.
If I could fly, I would fly away as a bird to her resting place,
Wailing all my flock breathing back our nesting place,
Lord, Your whisper lifted my soul from the depths of silence,
as I trust our destination.
Come, Lord, as the wind, in the wave, mighty God, in all Your
works.
Only You know how many times Your breath brought me back to
life.
No one saw my sinking ship; Your breath within me lifted me up
from my woeful plight!

Ipolita Sanchez
Brooklyn, NY

World Series Season

This time of year, baseball reigns.
Teams and players reach for optimal gains.
Only the elite play in October.
Make too many errors and your season is over.
The World Series is the ultimate goal.
Fielders and sluggers all play their role.
The best four out of seven is very serious,
But perform well on the field and the crowd is delirious!
I am partial to the New York Yankees.
They just win and don't need "homer hankies."
The Bombers are on the verge of winning it all.
The Phillies stand in their way this fall.
One win away from baseball heaven,
A simple equation of four out of seven.

Tom E. Belcher
Allendale, NJ

Friendship

A timely kind word in a moment of need,
A word of caution that we need to heed,
A funny joke to brighten our day,
A reminder for one another to pray.
A true friend is with you through thick and thin,
One who cares when your heart is troubled within.
It's never too early or too late to call,
You lean on each other so neither will fall.
A hand to help you up when you're down,
A laugh to create a smile from a frown.
A hug to make it all seem all right,
A voice to reassure in daytime or night.
People may come and go in our lives
Quickly as waves come in with the tide,
The waves crash on the rocks and rush back out to sea,
This is not how friendship should be.
God gives us friends in so many moments
When we cannot go one more hour,
Like a lighthouse leading us home
As a very welcome source of His power.
A true friend will accept you,
Not perfect by far.
Your Maker's work in progress,
Just as you are.

Linda G. Swanson
Jacksonville, FL

Are You Ready?

Today is the day our Lord could come.
Could you stop and talk to Him,
Or would you haft to run?
Are you ready to leave this land,
Or are you ashamed to take
The Savior's hand?

His coming is so near.
He said for you to have no fear.
Fear not, for I am with you to the end,
Around each corner and around each bend.

Jesus restored my soul, so on to Heaven we will go
To walk on streets of purest gold,
To walk by the sea of purest glass.
You'll never remember anything of the past.

When we get to Heaven, you see,
We'll get to sit down with the Savior
By the crystal sea.
See our loved ones who gone on afore,
Never to leave Heaven, never no more

Darlene Combs
Huntersville, NC

Jessie James

Long ago, when the west was young,
There lived a man, a rancher's son
Who turned out to be the fastest gun in the west.
Yes, Jessie James laid many a man to rest.
They called Jessie cold hell,
Bullets and flames.
Yes, everyone knew Jessie James.
He was a man who meant what he said
And backed it up with lead of bloody red.
He was a man of cold steel, fire, and lead
That others tried to outdraw, but died instead.

Gene R. Abner
Sadieville, KY

Time Is Becoming Short

I didn't think I would last this long time,
But here I am still, full of life and zest.
Thank You, God, for giving me Your very best.
My goodness, I know You didn't have to do it.
I have put myself in jeopardy more than I can count,
But there You were, pulling me out.
Thank You, God, that's what I am talking about.
I am now sixty-six and as I have said before,
Still full of life and why, I don't know.
It's not that I took so good care of myself,
It was You, oh, God, that has been caring for my health.

Melvin Hatter Jr.
Gary, IN

Public Pain

I go to my safety place, but you are not there.
It is known to me that you won't be there, but still I look,
Searching, hoping, wishing in vain.
Everywhere there is evidence of your existence,
Yet you no longer exist.
Mighty things you have done.
How were you unable to notice?
Shoulders wide and embracing.
Smile, so warm and comforting.
Stature, tall and protecting.
Never were you without a smile on your face.
Did it hurt to smile only when you were in public?
For your pain, there must have been no smiles when you were alone.
Poetic, that it was the heart.
Courteous, that it was in the garage in a sweatshirt.
Sad that such family love could not overcome.

Jeanne L. Huber Morr
Delaware, OH

The poet's brother, Lyle, left by freewill in March 2005 after an eighteen-year struggle with bipolar disorder. "Public Pain" is an attempt to understand how bipolar disorder can have control over warm, loving, outgoing, caring, and loved people such as Lyle. Hopefully the poem will help people to understand that mental illness isn't a disease of some stranger. It can happen to the friendly, outgoing person next door as well. "Public Pain" should be a lesson to always reach out to others, even if they appear to be in total control.

Dare to Dream

What wonders may yet be seen
When we pause and dare to dream
To hold one thought and make it your own
To grab onto hope and brave the unknown
Like fisherman finding a bountiful stream,
We cast our nets upon the water and dream
I am a slave, who was once a king
I am a vocalist, born to sing
I am a teacher, builder, soldier, priest
I can tap dance for you all night or prepare a gourmet feast
I am a scientist, inventor, farmer, father
I am a doctor, lawyer, diplomat, mother
Artist, athlete, astronaut, poet
I am a great orator who delivered a speech you will never forget
And from those words was spawned an historic event
From "I have a dream" comes a Black American president
We were first
And we shall outlast
So embrace your joy
And celebrate our past
What wondrous things might yet be seen
If we pause and dare to dream

Michael M. Jones
New York, NY

Anticipation

It is always an honor
Each time that I read or hear
How about sending a poem
But first, let us make ourselves clear.
This is an amateur contest,
it must not exceed twenty-four lines.
Won't you show us your artistic talent
All of the words in rhyme must be mine.
Oh, but I don't have anything prepared,
Maybe I'll just let this one pass me by,
But it seems, long before I even know it,
My mind begins working, causing a twinkle in my eyes.
I could be writing about a devastating heartache,
A heavy dew icily shining on a collapsing bush,
The exquisite breathtaking beauty of a double rainbow,
Or the absolute quiet of the early morning hush.
I know that this poem is strange and different
But I have written it especially for you.
Thank you for the opportunity, Eber and Wein.
Did I show that I can write a poem on cue?
As I anticipate the awaited assessment
And as you discuss my writing ability as a whole,
I am sure that I will be on pins and needles.
Denied can prick a poet's very delicate soul.

Patricia A. Crowder
Marion, NC

Love Poem

My life was nothing
until your sweet presence
breathed the breath of love
into my soul.

David Luciano
Cherry Hill, NJ

Ode to a B.M.

Oh, how I hear that little phrase.
I guess it will haunt me
Till my dying days.
"Did you have a bowel movement today?"
I have heard it every day, it seems
I even hear it in my dreams.
Oh, I know it would be the devil to pay.
If I missed a bowel movement one day.
They ask so sweetly, so concerned,
But it really makes my blood burn.
Oh, dear Lord, I pray
Don't let me miss my bowel movement today!

Mary R. Walden
Mt. Airy, NC

A Story About a Girl

This is a story
about a young girl
whose life was taken away
by a war
near her home.

The days go by,
no food, no water, no gas, no electricity.
She sleeps by a candle,
which lights only hope,
hope for which the war ends,
and peace is restored once more.

As her life goes by,
hope grows more,
once, a few,
then the world.

Liberation comes,
she leaves.
What keeps her together,
are two things . . . love and hope.

Tyler L. Koszewski
Holyoke, MA

Homecoming

Motherland, wipe your tears
I've been away for hundreds of years
Surviving, enduring in two
Parallel worlds—yours and mine.

I took a journey hundreds of years ago
Leaving the Cape, the Horn, and the Coast
Lured to some strange land I didn't know.

Since then,
I've grown strong.
I've learned a new tongue and forgot my own.
I brought the seeds of Africa
And planted them here.
Strong seeds—enduring seeds.

I now return to you, but
Things have changed.
People have changed;
I don't know if I recognize anyone anymore.

I'm still on that journey around the Cape, the Horn, and the Coast,
Lured back to the homeland, not a strange land,
To one I once knew,
To something that is familiar.

Violet D. Mensah
Poughkeepsie, NY

My Innocence

She's everything to me and barely two feet tall,
She's my innocence, what's left of it all.
Tiny little hands, rosy little cheeks,
A heavenly little spirit, going on twelve weeks.
Upon my softened heart has been left a lasting imprint
With a gentle little tiptoe and a tiny little footprint.
She looks into my eyes, gives me her precious smile,
Makes me understand why everything's worthwhile.
She's everything that's real . . . pure, honest, and true.
Has me wrapped around her finger—arms and ankles too!
Every moment, every minute,
Is priceless when she's in it.
Every second she's away leaves a feeling of dismay.
That's my little girl,
She's my heart, my soul . . . my world.
From the very first time I saw her
And every moment ever since,
My life has been forever changed
By the angel of innocence.

Amanda M. Morelli-Blanda
Aliquippa, PA

The Unknown

There they sit all in a row
Watching the pond put on its show

Every time I am here, I see them meet
All lined up in their regular seat

They have lived their lives and are old and gray
Now they can relax, watching the day

Geese are stretching, floating by with ease
Trees are letting everyone enjoy the breeze

The waterfall gives a spray and a thrill
They just keep sitting, blending into the hill

Sun comes out and shines light a light
Its a perfect day and feels so right

Once in a while, you hear a far cry
You listen and keep wondering why

These souls come here and sit alone
I'll always remember them as the unknown

Linda A. Baton
Dushore, PA

You Can Cry in the Rain

I was walking down the street when I passed you by
And saw teardrops in your eyes
You tried to look the other way
When I caught a smirk upon your face
As you disappeared around the corner without a trace
You were crying in the rain
No one could see your pain
You thought you could hide and not be found
Well I caught you before you got on that crazy train
You have changed that rainy day forever
With someone who cares
Angels are singing
Have faith
Stop your heart from breaking
Be strong
Do not let the evil get a hold of you
It is okay to cry in the rain
So do not have any shame

Sonia Altersitz
Deptford, NJ

Among the Shadows

A shade is what I am, invisible to the naked eye.
Living among the shadows.
Walking around for eternity, alone.
Overcome with nostalgia while watching love spread.
Wanting to move forward and embrace.
Wanting to know a loving touch once more.
Instead, I retrogress and cling on darkness.
The thought of feeling whole is simply preposterous.
Misery incinerated most of my senses.
Unfortunately, she is all I have ever since . . .
After being hoodwinked by people in guises
Whom I've once trusted.
Even now their gibes reiterate in my skull.
Once a forsaken angel who waited, now a shade
Who wishes to be seen and loved.
Trust me.
A voice? Not once has anyone ever spoken to me.
Following the voice, I found a man.
He too is a shade with bright sapphire eyes!
He asked for trust; happily, I accepted it.
The man who lived in the shadows.
The woman who lived in the shadows
Are no longer alone,
For they are visible to each other.

Kayla M. Funez
Buzzards Bay, MA

Two of a Kind

They said we would not make it,
but they were wrong.
They said we were different like night and day,
but we stood strong.
They said we had two different lifestyles,
but we learned how to maintain.
We were different in each other's eyes,
or was it society's opinion that told us a lie?
The only way we could have been together was if we both died.
Two hearts that were strong broke down by the world,
telling us we were not the same.
We were two of a kind that could have made it,
all we had to do was stay alive.
We let society take control and they let us die.
They said we would not make it and they were right.
We killed ourselves before we saw the light.

Ricardo Couch
Waverly Hall, GA

Bitterness

Clawing demon of the soul,
Acid in the deepest part
Boiling over memories past,
Poison oozing from the heart.
Seething over damage done
Pondering, living in the slime—
Lucifer, the outcast one,
Strokes this killer of our time.
Hissing in the inner man
Is the viper coiled to bite.
Surrendered to a life of hate,
A soul descends into the night.
Bitterness has done its work:
An ugly vagabond is born.
A life is forfeited to revenge;
Life is lived, no light of morn.

Kenneth N. Bullard
Bremen, GA

Birth and Death

The media of exchange from existence to existence
Are multifarious and estranged from mortal breath,
But the two that make a showing,
And seem somewhat within our knowing,
Are the ones we classify as birth and death.

As this soul takes on and sheds us in its universal jaunt,
I hope its next shell will be morally rich
So the glory that it wins
Will not be stacked with sins,
And its expulsion will be meritorious to a stitch.

Until the mind is deemed quite worthy
To plot the journey of the soul,
And absolution through reincarnation is left bereft,
We'll stick with God and His solution,
Keep a vigil eye on evolution,
And learn all we can of birth and death.

Howard H. Mackey Jr.
Edgewater, MD

Redbird

Pale blue shadows
Fall amidst the bitter snow
Broken limbs, tattered skin
Warding off the sun's glow

The grey bird watches
No longer taking flight
He always feels my pain
Through every sleepless night

My soul cries for comfort
Like a tired and lonely tree
Abandoned by her autumn leaves
Winter lives inside of me

So I watch from my window
As I sing a gentle hum
Waiting in my darkness
For my redbird to come

Carrie L. Smith
Douglas, MA

Little Monkeys

Little monkeys living in the woods came to hunt for food
Little children came looking for fun asked
Little monkeys, what are you doing here?
You are not responding
Since you cannot talk to us, then show us a sign
Are you dangerous or can we become friends?
Can we get close and touch you without hurting us?
Oh, little monkeys, are you so hungry you cannot talk?
We have been told to fear those things that do not respond
We guess you are hungry
Bye before you make a meal out of us

Ihuoma Enemuo
Jamaica, NY

Love

Sitting in the tall green grass in a meadow
On a beautiful summer morning as the
Morning breeze blows by
As my toes relax in the morning dew
As the winds blow, love is on my mind
While in the tall green grass
But is this a feeling or a intent for love
Taking over my mind in the meadow
Or is love what I'm really looking for
Love is a mystery, just like the wind
Love is . . .

Ricky D. Timbers
Midland City, AL

The Magician

She could feel his black magic
in the tips of her toes
in the tips of her fingers
in the sweat on his nose

In the shift of his tone
in the bend of his knee
in the nape of his neck
as he caressed her tenderly

In the glare in his eye
in the taste of his kiss
in the music he made
in his sensuous twist

She could sing
she could cry
she could swim
she could fly

But the magic he drew
like the sole of a shoe
wore to the thread
as he rose from her bed
and walked on and on and on.

Winifred S. Eure
Maplewood, NJ

Autumn Patchwork Quilt

Mother Nature made an autumn patchwork quilt for all the world to
see.
Jack Frost, her assistant, worked magnificently.
Changing rolling hills, mountains colors of every hue.
Hilltop observations, a breathtaking view.
A coverlet of colors, red, yellow, orange, varying shades of green,
a glorious rural scene.
Farmers plowing meadows, contrasting patches of light tan and
brown,
Nature's autumn patchwork quilt from earth producing ground.
Neatly piled stalks of cornfields, pumpkins at their side.
Stark white church steeples, a sense of country pride
Stretching in an endless sky of blue.
Red barns, white fences set askew
Blended a colorful patchwork quilt theme.
A rustic covered bridge over a reflecting autumn stream,
Gazed upon as every artist's dream.
White puffy clouds hiding sunshine,
Spotlights heighten a hidden color scheme.
A picturesque coverlet of originality,
Mother Nature performing her peak of autumn creativity.

Conrad Kipp
Dover Plains, NY

Yesterday Mourning

Every morning another yesterday
Our only shared interest
A 401K
Even the July sun cannot melt
The ice cold blanket that sheets
Our flannel pajama-clad bodies.

You sit silently
At the kitchen table
Sipping your morning cup of freshly brewed coffee
While reading the *Wall Street Journal*
The Dow Jones is
Down
Another day!
I watch a new episode of *As the World Turns*
The Daily Show is in reruns.

Emptiness
Fills our house with the smell of burnt toast
I open the refrigerator door
And pour pitchers of iced coffee
That I drink while smoking cartons of Camels
And daydream of sipping martinis in Tahiti
While dancing naked on the beach.

Sylvia Schuster
Huntington, NY

Short Temper

Is it something buried deep inside,
Something far beyond the soul and the heart?
Is it hurt and bitterness
That you can't control?

I am bitter and I am hurt,
But I don't kick and I don't strike.
I don't push against the wall.
I have a soul and a heart.
I have control.

I don't ever curse, I don't even judge.
I have a soul and a heart.
I have self-respect and respect for all.
I have control.

Eleni Voyages
Bayside, NY

Untitled

I regret the words I've said to you
with every passing day
Oh how I wondered why your wounds
clouded your eyes with hate
Now if I knew the revenge you'd seek
I'd take all the pain away
but if you think it's greater than mine
my help is beyond your reach

Amber J. Larson
Purgitsville, WV

Peace in the World

White clouds glide gracefully
Across the big blue sky
There was not a sign of rain
Or thunderstorm in sight
The yellow sun shone brightly
High in the heavens
Herds of sheep and longhorn cattle
Graze lazily in the meadows
Children played with glee and finally
The world was happy
And the voice of angels trembled
Like the sound of a symphony

Clive McKenzie
Neptune, NJ

Politicking Politicians

Radioactive dust now fills my lungs, I'm told not to worry,
It's safe; safe enough to eat with my breakfast cereal.
Tasteless, odorless, so small it can't be seen by the naked eye.
Its given name, depleted uranium, is misleading in itself,
to say the least.

Depleted—devoid, scantiest, smallest, lowest degree,
all to indicate lacking worth, useless, worthlessness.
As I sit, pondering the lies, why a misleading name now
describes a poison flowing through my veins.
Stuck to my bones as veterans sound the horns as a warning.
Depleted uranium, the Agent Orange of today's warrior.
Thirty years later, lies continue to flow,
flow from lips as water from a rushing stream.
Lobbyists pushing money from hand to hand
as if they were dreams.

A wanton disregard for our soldiers' lives
as they serve their country with duty, honor and pride,
unknowingly being betrayed by politics' oldest competition,
money, power, greed;
how will they ever succeed?

Herbert R. Reed
Columbia, SC

I've been married to a lovely lady named Colette Dawn Callender-Reed for fifteen grand years of love and friendship. We have two children, a daughter, Cymone Marie, and a son, Cortney Charles, who were conceived through love. The inspiration for this particular piece of poetry comes from my experience in Iraq as a soldier, and subsequently, dealing with various congressmen and senators regarding depleted uranium used by the U.S. and Great Britain in the war. Simply breathing highly contaminated air is enough to test positive for exposure to depleted uranium. The people elected to protect us from foreign and domestic terrorists have failed. Individuals having a working knowledge of DU sat quietly, knowing another person was walking into harm's way.

Reality: Shaken, Not Stirred

When I was younger, I learned how hard it would be
To elect a president with the same skin tone as me.
A female candidate would surely never be,
But I knew we lived in the land of the free.
So much hate and prejudice in 2009,
More people in unemployment lines.
Obama wins the Nobel Peace Prize
Shaken, not stirred across both party lines.
We pinch pennies and use coupons, which are fine,
The economy must change or I'll lose my mind.
We stand up to defend our rights through fear
With clinched fists while fighting back tears.
My dreams of attending college are no more,
Reality stepped in and closed that door.
I work two jobs while cutting back,
Looking for that one job with a benefits pack.
Favoritism in the workplace, I see it every day
How does one cope while earning their pay?
I want to believe in the American dream,
But life is not always what it seems.
I will do my best through poetry and word.
Forget what you've heard,
For I will forever remain shaken, not stirred.

Angel A. Fulford
Laurel, MD

Darkness

Darkness surrounds all, living in everyone.
You can see it in the eyes of the children.
Sometimes it's just a shadow
in the corners of the world.

Some days, darkness and light can be balanced.
You start to think that the light will prevail,
but in the flash of a second, the darkness
engulfs all that you care about.

To have one there is always another.
Always living in everything you know.
You can hear it and see it; sometimes it's small,
other times, it can create war.

It spreads slowly, engulfing the world,
sometimes one person at a time.
Other times, a whole city or even a nation,
slowly at first, then quickly till all is lost.

Tommie L. Wertenberger
DeFuniak Springs, FL

Master

I wait in the shadows
Chestnut waves upon the pillow
I watch as he surreptitiously take her honor
I listen as she demeans her
Patience wins my goal
Escape is not possible
Each day my gripe grows stronger
Eradicate the light, I shall
Control and guard my daily labor
I am mighty
I have power
My prey consumed
I will have her for my own
Her life is mine
Her light grows dim
As my darkness encroaches
My ebony becomes deeper
A void where only I exist
For I know her story
From the beginning I was there
The story is my key
Ever present I turn the key and I enter
I am Master—I am fear
I am beyond defeat!

Florence T. Compher
Hammonton, NJ

When I Go Back Home Again

Of all the places where I've lived
and places where I've been,
not one can I call my own
until I go back home again.
The home place of my childhood
is much different from back then,
yet there's the fence and the old oak tree
to welcome me home again.
I am in awe as I look around, taking in a precious view
as if I were there, so young, when my life was new.

Sweet memories, how they touch me when I'm all alone,
not of people that I've met or places where I've been.
It is such a sweet sensation
when I dream of going back home again.
I recall the days of laughter, I recall the many tears.
My memories have not faded in all the many years.

Days are drawing closed, dear sister.
Only two of us are left to share
the memories of our childhood,
the love of our kin, and our love for each other
when I go back home again!

Sandra E. Gallardo
Linton, IN

Anyone

My crown may be a bit tarnished
But it's shiner then ever.
My eyes are still bright and shiny,
But they don't see all they used to.
My thirty-two white horses on a red hill
Have diminished and some have been lost in battle.
My shoulders are still broad and proud,
But now they sag and are tired.
My legs aren't as they once were
Now they are tired, ache, and sore.
My knees don't bend like they used to,
Getting up has become a chore.
My feet aren't as fast as they used to be,
But they still get me from point A to B.
As I look at life dawn the road,
I still carry a heavy load,
When I was young, the golden years seemed so far away.
What I didn't know was the gold was only tarnished rust.

Carl E. Gutilla
Pittsburgh, PA

More

"Someone" kept a journal
In hopes to find a prize.
He dared not blink, lest he
Should miss the "more" before his eyes.
"More" may come as strangers,
Some have lost the way.
Others came to look around,
But never meant to stay.
Travels took "Someone" to
A land beyond the shore,
Where every journal hoped to record
The heart of the land called "More."

A well lay in a barren land,
Which once was named "Hope."
As sail was turned and "Someone" found
And wove dead fibers he called "rope."
The years passed on as "Someone" with Hope,
Yearned for a place they might belong,
But lying there at "Someone's" feet
Were the fibers Time made strong.
Each time "Someone" would take the soil,
Removing all of the sand,
He would smile and rest in hopes,
Praying, "This is the 'More,' the land."

Kathleen A. Hynes
Largo, FL

About to Fall

Days are long—nights are hard
My faith is gone—my heart is scarred
The voices loud—the tears I cry
My greatest fear—I'm not sure why
Illusions seem so real
Illusions like the emotions that I feel
I remember the nights so cold
Reliving the days of old
The terror unrefined
The meaning of love redefined
His touch ever seeking
A mouth used for more than speaking
Sometimes bruised—sometimes swollen
The worst pain—a childhood stolen
No one there—no one to tell
Trapped in a prison—my solitary cell
Who is there to help me—is there hope at all
Who is there to catch me as I am about to fall

Tina M. Bealer
Uniontown, OH

Why?

So many wonders
And so many questions
I sit alone, by myself
And I ask myself
Why do things have to be so complicated?
Why do people have to die?
Why does God make some people suffer
While other people smoke reefer?
Sometimes I want to die
And sometimes I want to hide
And sometimes I just want to cry
Why does the world have to be so messed up?
Why can't Obama make things right?
Why do so many people have to fight?
Why do so many people have to separate?
Why can't we all just be together?
Can anyone answer me?

Laura M. Spatney
Mantua, OH

Lay

Across the field and down the hill, his trek takes him far.
This common stride, aspiration high, nary known his heart.
Midst tempest's pour sought shelter before malady claimed his form.
Cavernous mine, utopian hide from the sudden wild storm.
Securely inside and soon to find himself not the only incumbent,
He shares his space with a handsome face, never seeing its
semblance.
Her eyes' gaze in surplus and haze read oddly soothing to him.
Returning her gleam, sea glass green eyes kindle and penetrate skin.
Communication commenced with questions of whence.
Introductions needn't be wrought.
Identity known, all but shown. Mannerisms needn't be sought.
She too, this young lass of satin, of glass
Whilst jaunting along in the meadow,
Required lee of the mine, utopian hide from the atmospheric bellow.
Discourse progresses; tales of obedience, transgressions.
Not a detail slips from their memoir.
Every word spoken, a lingual token taken to remember.
Amorous talk ceases as harsh weather eases.
These kindred souls burn sooth.
Each can't discern of want, of yearn; their passion, not uncouth.
This eternal twain, love simple and plain
Confirmed by a single request.
This man mesmerized by her radiant eyes put their hearts to the test.
"I pledge thee, my troth, a sacred oath in this utopian hide;
Henceforth, shall I live to nourish,
to cherish my wondrous Earth-dolven bride."

Samantha L. Winkler
Chambersburg, PA

Privileged

Privileged to be allowed to visit with patients on four floors
once a week for thirteen years as a volunteer

Privileged to bring some aid and comfort to patients
and see newborns and new mothers together for first time

Privileged to be able to sew operating cloths,
mother's pad and X-ray robes to be used by patients

Privileged to be able to work alongside nuns who
have set up hospitals for the sick poor and newborns
and unwed mother facilities

They have made places for everyone,
especially our wonderful volunteers

Nuns have also staffed schools where they taught
reading, writing, mathematics, religion and moral values
We can't forget music and poetry

Where would we be without them? Not so privileged.

Mary E. Soley
Seaford, NY

I was prompted to write this poem about the thirty years I volunteered at Mercy
Medical Center in Rockville Center, Long Island, New York. I enjoyed all aspects
of work but especially enjoyed and felt privileged to be able to go up on all four
floors of the hospital visiting patients. We brought the outside world to them with
a cart that contained books, magazines, prayer cards, greeting cards, candy, snacks,
stuffed animals, and also some clothing, jewelry, and baby clothes. This broke up
the daily routine of medication, food, and bathing. Patients liked to talk to someone
especially if an article on the cart invoked happy memories.

Gone

Oh, how I wish that you were here
To guide me on my way
To care for me and comfort me
And get me through the day

I miss the times we used to sit
And talk for hours on end
Oh, how I wish that you were here
So we could do it all again

The words I say are blown away
In the howling of the night
The tears I've cried have said goodbye
To loveless, sleepless eyes

I miss you more than words could say
Or love could ever know
There's nothing now that I can do
To ever let you know.

Aylia M. Holmes
Youngstown, OH

Geminian Aquarius

Dramatic flair was always your strongest trait
Effervescent attributes which were passed on to both your offspring
Basically allowing all your family to possess those necessary facets
Originally showing everyone the most unusual aspect known to man
Rarely failing at whatever task that you decided to attempt
Always displaying the most positive gestures
To each acquaintance and friend
Hanging around with everybody you had known your whole life
through
Assurance brought about an unusual situation very recently
Never seeing any negative gesture brought against you today
Nobody decided to perform so unruly a feat for no reason at all
Explanations abounded by everybody you had known so well
Triumphant at all the tasks you decided to undertake
Rewarding each individual that you knew with positive traits
Endurance was another facet which you possessed abundantly
Yearning to pass all of it on to both of your siblings
Because that fact would have been known to even your adversaries
Always bringing forth the best gesture known to all
Listing the most unusual ever seen in this landscape
Leisurely causing the strongest attribute to return in spades

Richard R. Perna
Neptune, NJ

Under the Sea

Imagine you see world tranquility
In a land of richly colored coral
In true blissful glee deep under the sea
Where the sun's rays dim to just let things be
Eternally just so pictorial
Imagine you see world tranquility
Wide-eyed fish flash on their morality
Look closer now, their thoughts have a moral
In true blissful glee deep under the sea
Above, waves crash rocks 'til infinity
But here is a place where none will quarrel
Imagine you see world tranquility
An octopus curls out so happily
While anemones glee deep under the sea
This awesome place leads us so readily
To want to stay in this place pastoral
In true blissful glee deep under the sea
Imagine you see world tranquility

Janice E. Lawrence
Bridgewater, MA

I Am Only Me

I am only me, that is all I can be
No more, no less, I laugh and I cry
I've wished at times, that I could fly!
Some days I'm funny, other I'm not,
Sometimes I'm in overdrive and can't stop.
I am a loyal and honest friend,
You know that I'll be there until the end.
I am a father / mother to my children,
My greatest gift!
The smiles on their faces always gives me a lift
I am a romantic, sensual, sexual,
And passionate too,
To the love of my life, I'll share this with you.
I can be sweet and shy or sassy and bold.
I'm quite a handful, or so I've been told.
I am not perfect, I do have my faults
Like when I get scared, I put up high walls
Or I'm not as forgiving, as I'd sometimes like to be,
Because when I hurt, I hurt deeply.
My logic is all my own, at times misunderstood,
Because I don't always do things for my own good.
I have many facets, like a diamond you see...
I am only me!

Stella M. Neglia
Lincroft, NJ

In Remembering the 1.2 Million Children

In remembrance of
The 1.2 million children

We used to laugh.
We used to play.
We used to cry.

We played a game of dreidel.
Lit the menorah.
Danced the hora.
We ate unleavened bread.

Nor can we ever hear
The Shofar

Blowing in
Our Jewish New Year.

In our homeland
We were separated
From our families
By Hitler and his Nazis.

We are the 1.2 million children
That were loved,
Netted into slavery

With hard labour,
Never to be free.

We have all perished.
Remember us in May
On Holocaust Day.

Gwenyth Jenkinson
Port Chester, NY

Pray

Sometimes as children we fight
when we want to get our way.
My mom taught me a better way,
get down on your knees and pray.

You might not get what you ask for.
You may think He did not hear.
He sends only what is best for you
and it is perfect and clear.

God's ears are always listening,
His eyes are never closed.
Don't be like the child who
fights to get his way.
Do what my mom taught me to do,
get down on your knees and pray.

Helen C. Evans
Bucksport, ME

The Team Slump

Their pitcher's striking men out at the plate,
Their shortstop's snatching fly balls from the air;
Their long-ball hitter pounds one to the gate,
And you believe the ump's call wasn't fair.
You're sure your team will not survive a year
Of series games against teams good and bad.
What you could do to win is not so clear,
The fix your team is in makes fans so mad.
The team will need some help, so start with luck,
And cash, esprit, and longer practice days.
Then add some requisites you cannot duck,
Like prayer and magic spells that would amaze.
If you could stir all these into the pot,
Your team (you hope), can once again be hot!

Vincent M. Lombardi
New York, NY

I've written prose and poetry for pleasure on and off for years, but I believe the writing and reading of poetry offers both writer and reader the greatest rewards. This sonnet, as well as several others, was written for my granddaughter, who recently asked me about various kinds of poetry, and in particular, about Shakespearean sonnets. I saw her inquiry as an opportunity for me not only to teach her something valuable about poetry in general, but also to illustrate firsthand the inherent difficulties and personal rewards of composing a sonnet specifically in a modern idiom.

Lord, Lift Me Up

Lord, lift me up, for I don't always have the strength
to hold up my faith, courage, and hope in You.
I get discouraged very easily
and I know that You are in my heart and soul,
but I don't always accept You
because of the downfalls in my life,
and that I get put down a lot
because I'm not as smart as I should be.
I know deep down that You have forgiven me for my faults.
How can I keep on believing that You're with me
when I sometimes disbelieve in myself?
I'm going to church every week and taking in Your Word
and asking for help in my work.
Am I asking for too much from You, Lord?
Am I asking in the right way, Lord?
I do get discouraged very easily.
Is that okay, to get discouraged at times?

Diana G. Woodsum
Auburn, ME

To Have It As It Was

You've never said it
In so many words.
I'm feeling what you're thinking,
Though it's never heard!

Done all the things
That should've let you know
Just how you make me feel,
How much I love you so!

So you've gone away,
Leaving me all alone,
Left without no one
I can call my own.
What goes around comes around,
As it always does,
But I would do anything
To have it as it was!

Lillie M. Pennington
Coatesville, PA

Remember

There are things in life that help you remember.
The smell of a flower in a warm spring day.
The touch of a kiss from a child's happy face.
The music on a record heard long ago.
The smile of a friend found all over again.
The light of the sun, shining bright in the sky.
The look of a man admiring a loving wife.
The face of a mother, caring for her child.
The feeling of pride when they've done something right.
The joy of a father when teaching his son to drive.
The sound of children's laughter on a merry-go-round.
The pink rosy color of your baby's cheeks,
The way that you feel at you child's graduation.
The hurt when they decide it's time to leave.
The emptiness when they're long gone.
The darkness is coming, so remember it all,
Because these are the things that should be remembered.

Luzeady Cuadrado
Philadelphia, PA

The Other Side

These words are for the poor child who is left behind
Fragile one with dirt on the face and a brilliant mind
Seeking direction from someone that never seems to come
All the while standing still but always on the run

For the man who awakes each morn on a bed of stone
Always wanting to be loved but ends the day helpless and alone
Reaching out his cup for a small amount as people take a glance
Looking towards the deep blue sky begging for one more chance

My future of endless hours in a concrete box counting time
As I try to salvage my tarnished reputation in a six-by-nine
Longing for the day when these walls will be behind me
A trail of mistakes haunt me deep inside I will never be free

Thoughts and memories all fill our delicate minds
Some we welcome and some are not so kind
Things we embrace come and soon shall pass
As we all struggle and fight to grab the ring of brass

Daniel V. Shaffer
Galloway, OH

Dance with the Devil

Comfortable and cozy in my den
Luna beckons me to join her children
Inside me debating and deciding I might
I run and play in the firefly light
I'm led to a world to see the devil himself
Dancing and laughing, forgetting myself
I can't help, my resolve is melting
He's so beautiful, alluring, and tempting
His taunting and teasing are too much to bear
Clouding my mind, I know I should beware
I should've stayed in away from the night
But curiosity took me and calmed my fright
Temptation aplenty, I fight for the power
In hopes that the sun will shine this hour
He asks me to dance on the tip of the stars
Burning my hand, we cha-cha to Mars

Melody M. Ranck
Harrisburg, PA

Arrived Late

On the dirt road, carriage is drawn by two horses.
Dogs ran, but could not keep up with the horses.
To move faster coachman softly whip horses' backs.
To a remote town the traveler wishes to get soon.
Coachman asks which way to turn, left or right?
"Go straight ahead." He left town fifty years ago,
doesn't remember which way to turn, left or right.

As world traveler seldom visited his birth town,
he said, "Find the cemetery." The caretaker says,
"Your mother died yesterday, is buried next to your
father." He whispers, "Why no cross on graves?"
Then remembers as child with his religious father,
they went to the synagogue, his mother, the local
rabbi's daughter, observed Sabbath and holidays.

The sun went down, the moon shines, the sky with
bright stars. Wish to pray for his death parents,
but remembers only one world. "Jiszgadal," repeats,
"Jiszgadal, Jiszgadal." Places some change in the
donation box and heartbroken walks out from the
cemetery, thinks why did not come sooner to see
his parents while they were alive.
Sits in the carriage and tells the coachman, "Let's go fast."
Wished to see his parents, but arrived too late.

Elly Gross
Jamaica, NY

Sixty-Seven Years

We've been together for so long
and through it all we were strong.

But those sixty seven years
have been reduced to falling tears.

A young man walks in,
you ask about him.

I say, "He is our son,
We cared for him when he was young."

Now he's here to help me take care of you
because he knows it's too much for me to do.

I show you a picture,
you ask of who.
I say with a smile
"This is me, and that is you."

Holding each other on our wedding day
and every day we still embrace,
but only because of God's grace.

Now we walk little walks
and we talk faint little talks.

And I kiss you good morning like I always do
as I softly whisper, "I love you."

Jeffrey M. Bennett
St. George, VT

I am a native of Vermont. I have two sons, Joshua and Andrew. All of my poetry comes from things I have experienced or witnessed throughout my life. I wrote this poem after speaking with a visitor in the hospital where I work. We talked about his wife and her battle with dementia.

The Swimming Hole

The sun comes up and beats down with a burning heat
You can feel your heart pound with a rhythm that repeats
It looks like diamonds sparkling from the water's reflection
As it bounces around from the rays of the hot summer sun
The sounds from the swimming hole can make your ears start
    ringing
The frogs are croaking, bees buzzing and the birds are singing
The white sand on the bottom gleams through to show you the way
As on the old rope with the tire swing you jump, push, and sway
You drop down with a resounding splash into the water of the pool
And your body sinks deep into the sandy bottom that is so cool
It only takes a few minutes to become refreshed, you see
Because the water is colder than you think it could be
You hold your breath as you dive and send up a big splash
Then you swim to the shore faster than a hundred-yard dash
You climb out on the grassy bank and fall on the blanket so hot
And lie on your back to dry, gazing at the clouds floating aloft
There is nothing so fine to ease your body on a hot summer day
Than a trip to the old swimming hole for an hour or two of play

Carole H. Auton
Hickory, NC

Delay to Your Love Reaction

Delay to your love reaction.
His love is just a little delay.
His love is always a desire.
Delay to your love reaction.
No matter how hard
I try to love you,
It's just a love reaction.

Stephanie E. Elder
Atlanta, GA

My name is Stephanie Elder. I am a Georgia girl—some may say a Georgia peach. I am a young artist who wants to be a writer. I have been writing for about ten years. The reason why I wrote this poem "Delay to Your Love Reaction" is because I want people to have a love poem to read to each other, the one they love in life. My mother is a substitute teacher. My father is a bus driver, and I am the oldest of three children. My sister, LaTrevia, and I are both in college, and my brother, Steven, is a student.

Empty

When I looked into your eyes, I could see a distant warmth.
When you wrapped your arms around me,
I could feel an essence or illusion of protection
calling me closer to you.
And when we kissed for the first time,
I felt the urgency, a hint of affection,
and all that passion buried inside.
But the last woman, all the other women that have come before . . .
before we met, stomped on the hope
and crushed the loving tenderness down
so far in your heart, it's hard to feel.
And now, now that God has finally brought into your life
that one and only soul mate, friend, and lover . . .
you're empty, you have nothing else to give to her
who soothes your heart and prays for your broken spirit,
who wants to ease your troubled mind
and comfort your finely chiseled physique.
And because you are unable or unwilling to give her,
the one you've searched for through all those other women,
the affection that she needs and the attention that lets her know that
he does want her in his life,
she who's holding on strictly by faith, will be gone!
Nothing but emptiness.

Janet M. Johns
Lithia Springs, GA

Wayfarer Sage

Around the mountain summit I saw him
Approach the little Alpine village green,
Then stop to look about through eyes made dim
By all the travel his years had seen.
A rustic, ruddy look was on his face
And all belongings in canvass on his back.
A walking staff in hand helped keep his pace,
A clock of seldom use was in the sack.

The region's legend he had become—
His story was of sojourns East and West.
These lonely ventures looked odd to some
The wisdom sought and gained convinced the rest.
They say he had unveiled the Orient
And knew a Hindu guru's teachings well,
Perused the knowledge of the Occident
And pondered the reaches of Heaven and Hell.

In awe, I raised a point to test his thought.
"Know others as you know yourself," he said,
And answering that for which I long had sought
He vanished then to where the rock path led.

Brent Webber
Brookneal, VA

Peace

Everyone desires peace
in one way or another,
whether it be a peace of mind,
or with their only brother.

Peace is a wonderful thing
in one way or another,
as it is every human's dream
from war or being smothered.

I find my peace looking in the sky
watching all the clouds go by,
and I wonder how I could bring it
to those who cry.

I have a dream to bring peace
to others and hope that I can try.
Peace is a wonderful thing
to make them have some peace before they die.

Regina R. Marino
Hamden, CT

Winter Gales

Wind-sculpted snow frosts the earth,
Like memory frozen over with time.
The air is sweet as maple candy,
The natural world has fallen silent.

Crumpled wool gray clouds
Filter the indifferent sun.
The year's last paper kite
Is caught up in the elm.

Clear ice across the sidewalk
Holds red and yellow leaves,
Gemstone colors of autumn
Encased for all to see.
Fresh rosettes of paw prints
On the crayon white hillside
Begin to blanket over
As snowflakes fill the sky.

It is a cold, cold thing,
This longing to remember,
Like the scolding of summer
Through the month of December.

Matthew R. Dow
Alexandria, VA

Look at the Sky

Look at the sky, dear
Look at it closely.
You will see brightness.
You will see colorful stars like us.
You will feel sweetness
That touches your skin.
It will make you feel beautiful
Like a morning rose.
Listen to the voices that whisper you kindly.
Sweetness, sun has touched your skin so gently.
Listen to the melody that sings about you.
Be kind and nice,
Let it take you to Heaven
And teach you how to fly.
Just be patient, and let the skies do the rest.

Suzanna S. Hakobyan
Brooklyn, NY

The Last Time

The last time
I traveled across the desert
The last time
I saw history falling down
The last time
I fired my best shot
The last time
I angled with masked men
The last time
I told you I would be victorious
The last time
My body was ready to fall apart
The last time
I was outnumbered
The last time
I dreamed of victory
The last time
I dreamed of her
The last time
I landed back on earth
For the last time.

Jason K. Thomas
Fayetteville, NC

Having moved from Virginia to North Carolina, my classes at college had to be put
on hold for a semester and I am in the process of writing a short story. After winning
third place in a poetry contest in college, I knew my dream to become a writer was
possible. My spare time is filled with writing. Writing gives me the feeling of
freedom, freedom of my thoughts.

A Heartbeat

A heartbeat.
Calming, comforting sound.
A new life.
A new mother.
A heartbeat.
Two becoming one.
Beating three times.
Skipping once.
Then continuing.
It says "I love you."
A heartbeat.
Connecting families.
Keeping them together.
Making a strong bond.
A heartbeat.
Linking pet and owner.
They will be bonded.
Through hardships
They will be each other's comfort.
A heartbeat.
Connecting all.
Through life and love.
The beginning of everything.
A heartbeat.

Veronica L. Smith
Richmond, ME

Sunset

Cradled against the evening skies,
Purple sorrow for the man who dies.
Red blood spilled for the sins of Man,
And framed in gold by God's own hand.
The blue of the sky in Mary's eyes
Mirrors sadness as she watches and cries.
Pink clouds of happiness say, "He is risen,"
The sins of Man have been forgiven!

Laurel M. Seymour
Needham, MA

Everyone enjoys a beautiful sunset, so I've taken the word "cradled" as a sign of His birth. In the central lines, agony on the cross and finally His glorious resurrection, so when one sees a sunset they will think of our Lord in thanksgiving for His great gift!

Dreams Come True

You say I made
Your dreams come true
But what I did
Was for me too

It's nice to know
What we share
Can add to life
And make us glad

If I give you
What you need
Then I can take
My needs too

To make a goal
And see it through
Then all anew
To share with you

New adventures
Around each bend
Would I have dared
If not for you

You push me on
With encouraging words
To do much more
Then on my own

Donna Downing
Thornton, NH

Couldn't You

Couldn't you just come back?
You can't impress me with a stack.

Couldn't you just remember
My birthday that's in December?

Couldn't you go back in time?
Would you commit a crime?

Couldn't you stop drinking?
I have been thinking.

Couldn't you go to a rehab?
You don't need to go blab.

Couldn't you just come back?
We could go canoeing and buy a kayak.

Couldn't you do better?
I guess you're too drunk to write a letter.

Couldn't you just come back?

Brandon T. Flowers
Hamilton, OH

The Bride's Deck of Cards

As you take the sacred vow on your wedding day,
Remember a deck of cards will guide you along the way.
Take hold of his hand like a lifeline to his heart.
A king and queen that never shall part.
The diamond reminds me of your love.
The ace as head of the household representing God above.
The deuce reminds me of love shared by two.
Three it will take (God, man, woman) to keep a promise of "I do."
The word "love," with letters of four—a marriage vow forevermore.
A total of five as the parents and two joined on one.
May life be good until life's journey is done.
The hour of six is the sunrise and the sunset,
A love growing since the two have met.
Seven is the magic number the Bible says to forgive.
Forgive over and over as long as the two shall live.
Eight is the exciting month to say "I do."
Joining two hearts starting life anew.
The number nine—the year that two lives become one.
The clock strikes ten—time for rest, the day is done.
I see the jack as the devil in disguise.
Let no intrusions interfere with newly joined lives.
Joker is a symbol too, things going wrong as they sometimes do.
Then you must take a deck of cards to remind you of love,
And your marriage will be blessed from God above.

Carol L. McKinney
Sullivan, IN

The Music in Me

How do I explain this rhythm in my brain?
This pounding eruption is driving me insane.
My love,
My passion,
The one that will remain.
The one that stays the same when everything starts to change.
I want to set it free, then maybe it will be
A glorious occasion when I am someone to be.
Its dying to burst out
In a whisper or a shout!
Or a tune with no vocals,
It's like my talent is in a chokehold.
And as it dashes through my mind, sometimes I want to cry,
Realizing that I may never reach my time to fly.
So this thing is not easy, you see,
I can never ignore the music within me.

Joseph T. Hampton
Toledo, OH

This Life Called Life

A dramatized world of effortless
Situations, memorized by thousand of teary
eyes, souls lost in a world of no solved
problems in this life called life.
Juveniles and dysfunctional turmoil
is justified to a memory lost to no return,
of a world that is traumatized of fear and pain
in this life called life.
Salvation of freedom, therefore
a strength that is so fully appreciated,
we all bow down to a god that can handle
any and all problems
in this life called life.
No selfish situations within our souls,
will neither be damaged by sinful thoughts
of no tomorrow, as we all suffer sometimes
in this life called life.
Tomorrow, we will brave the tide,
for God knows it will change;
situations of untold bravery and strength,
which will sear through eternity,
because things come in time due to
this life called life.

Carolyn Delk
Stanton, TN

Las Vegas Wedding

At the wedding chapel on the Las Vegas Strip
My son and his fiance's wedding, it was a trip!
Arriving at the wedding chapel
In a sleek white limousine,
Part of the package deal—
Service fit for a king and queen!
The wedding party was ushered in,
Five, including bride and groom.
The Elvis-looking preacher.
Quickly entered the room.
A few bars from "Here Comes the Bride"
Bride and groom stand side by side!
"Do you take this woman?"
"I do!"
"Do you take this man?"
"I do, too!"
"I now pronounce you man and wife!"
"Kiss the bride and get on with your life!"
"Here's a snapshot to remember this day!"
"Next, please!" the preacher exclaims
As the new bride and groom speed away!

Donald E. McKinney
Charlotte, NC

Alpha and Omega

Amongst all around, I feel your breath in the breeze
Carry me to content despite the disease
My entranced eager eyes fight for forgiveness
To give glory to Heaven and home, hosanna!

Impregnable innocence justified all jurisdiction
To know knowing know and love loving love
Mankind misinterprets nourishment as nothing
Often oppressing optimism to pursue pessimistic

Quivering lips question, "Is this right?"
Release, not revenge
Sustain strength through the strife

Testified to the truth in united understanding
With victorious voice we ask, "What's left to wonder?"
We've found our map's X

Yesterday's yearning now at an end
Today zealous in Zion, forever
Amen.

Robert D. Novack
Hope, NJ

The Perseverance of Life

How long will I hide my face?
How long will I long for the place
Where my enemy has lost his pace?
Oh, will I be able, with faith, to finish the race?
How long will I watch my dreams come to naught?
How long will I wrestle with the thought
That every day is a battle that must be fought?
For I'm not my own, I've been bought.
I must not find a permanent place here.
Give light to my eyes to stop the tears
So death will no longer be a fear.
I must, I will overcome, for time draws near.
My foe waits for me to grow weak.
He never tires of his endless seek
To prevail against me when life seems bleak,
But strong I will remain—unmovable, this I speak.
These words may seem spoken in vain,
For all know the just and unjust both get rain.
Fact: Life is not easy. This truth is plain.
The defining factor, does my life bear a blood strain?
When the blood is applied, it's the darkness that must hide.
The light now gives direction and a spring in the stride.
My strength is renewed. Now the tears that are cried
Are in humility for my possession of triumphant pride.

Dewana B. Overstreet
Selma, AL

A Fisherman's Paradise

A fisherman paradise,
I think would be fine.
A place of no worries,
Never pressed for time.

A place where big fish
Are the only ones caught.
A place where lies are not told
Of how long they are, or not.

When it comes to the weight,
It would be several pounds.
The story would be true
Whichever way it sounds.

The scrap books with clippings
From the news and sports magazines,
Your picture in bold print,
My, what joy. Oh, what dreams!

This paradise does exist,
Or so they do say.
It's a place where the big ones go
That have gotten away!

Kenneth C. Kincaid
St. Cloud, FL

Love Again

The circumstances of my past
Have led my heart astray
Which is why it is hard for me
To believe in what you say
The sweet words that leave your mouth
Make it hard for me to breathe
But I have to remember my wall
Because I'm scared you, too will leave
The confusion in my head
Makes me want to kick and scream
But every peaceful night
It is you in my dreams
And I want so bad to kiss you
To feel your arms hold me tight
But fear sets in, my head starts to spin
And I run when it feels too right
I hope you understand
That I am falling extremely fast
And beginning to trust
You will not repeat my past
For I will admit to this love
But don't ask me when
All I know for sure is
I will love again

Tabitha Hewitt
Brandon, MS

God-Given

Swim in the seas of my eyes
Feel my touch
Hold hands with my heart
Feel the kiss of my love
As it flows through your veins
You are the one I long for
The one I crave like my salvation
You are the grace in my spirit
The blessing in my soul
My God-given revelation
Your beauty, I behold
My love for you is read like a verse in Proverbs
Line for line and word for word
Gently sculptured by the hands of the Alpha and Omega
There is no love greater
Living deeply in you, you breathe through me
I'll sacrifice areas in my life to have you in mine
With no regrets or self-neglect
Hands cut off of those who bring forth harm
You are sacred
My blank page of endless possibilities
My lips are the pen
As I write over your body poetry

Monya L. Williams
Jacksonville, FL

A Ball Hit Foul

It wasn't Yankee Stadium
Or even Wrigley after dark
Just a makeshift diamond
In our neighborhood park
No bleachers or billboards framed our dusty field
Just majestic gardens bursting with their yield
Joe swung the bat a little late
The ball soared foul over the garden gate
Out ran an "old" man of at least forty years
His voice boomed on our young ears
"I'll throw it back, this time, it's free
But next time, boys, the ball belongs to me"
The calendar flips fast and hard
Now my grandsons play ball in our yard
Dom pitches to Vinny at the plate
He swings, the ball soars foul over the garden gate
I grab the ball and with a little glee
I echo the words once said to me
"I'm throwing it back, this time, it's free
But next time, boys, the ball belongs to me"
A sudden chill runs from my head to knee
As I realize the "old" man of long ago now is me.

Robert L. DiNardo
Schenectady, NY

365

The Sea

The smell of salt is in the air
The wind is gently blowing my hair
Sand slips away from under my feet
As the waves crash on the rocks all around me
It's amazing how such viscous force roaring in
Can at times be so calming
I ask as I look out at the deep blue sea
How does it bring the mind to peace and tranquility?
Surfers, divers, fishermen all love the sea
Fish of all kinds live in the underneath beauty
Tug boats and cruise liners at the harbors meet
Carrying cargo and passengers from country to country
Spectacular sunrises and sunsets like you've never seen
Lighthouses shine from port to port
Coastlines are filled with beach resorts
As I sit on the rocks at the beach
Looking out over the horizon for as far as I can see
And wonder how this body of water
Can be so mystifying, magical, and amazing.

Lynn A. LaDuke
Brimfield, MA

That Dress of Pale Blue

I dreamt of you, your pretty face I did see,
Remembered the very first time I saw you
Standing in the surf, dress held o'er your knee,
So beautiful you were in that dress of pale blue.

Our time together we could not surpass,
It was a joy so rare and all too brief;
Shattered like a broken wine glass,
Your death filled me with such grief.

The cop didn't see you, rammed your car,
Sent it into a pole where it broke in two.
You were dead before the ambulance got far,
Wearing that pretty dress of pale blue.

Oh, for the touch of your hand once more,
To run my fingers over your pretty face.
Oh, kiss your dear lips as before,
To touch your heart in that special place.

I dreamt of you once again last night,
And of that golden time I first saw you
There in the surf, that beautiful sight,
Standing there in that dress of pale blue.

All I have left are these thoughts of you
Wearing that pretty dress of pale blue.
All I can remember is that surf and you
Wearing that pretty dress of pale blue.

Carl W. Harris
Pittsgrove, NJ

Born in southern New Jersey, I have lived there most of my life. I have been writing for much of my life, and many of my poems tend to tell a story. I am a veteran of the air force and am married with three grown children and six grandchildren. My poem, "That Dress Was Pale Blue" was inspired by the aftermath of an auto accident. A New Jersey State trooper apparently ran a stop sign and collided with an oncoming car, killing both young female occupants. In my poem, I made this sad event a personal tragedy.

Who Was There?

Who was there on that holy night so long ago?
Who was lying in a manger bed of hay?
Who was watching over this sleeping baby?
Who was singing in the sky above?

Shepherds were there to see the baby in the stable
Jesus, God in the flesh, was lying in a manger bed of hay
Mary and Joseph were watching over the sleeping baby
Angels were singing praises to the newborn King

What was shining in the sky that night?
Who stood around the bed of hay?
Who came to visit from afar?

A star was shining so brilliant over this stable in Bethlehem
The cows and sheep and donkeys beheld the sleeping child
Magi brought gifts of gold, frankincense, and myrrh

Why did He come?
What did He come to do?

He came to save a lost and dying world
Redeeming work to save mankind

For whom?

For you and me!

Linda M. Burris
Cambridge, OH

Love Defined

Can love be defined?
A passionate feeling,
The need for life,
Or can love be defined
A broken heart
And caustic strife?

Do we live our life with love,
Together casting shadows
On the ground below,
Or do we cease love's contention,
Lonely in moonlight
With nothing to show?

Will love last?
The glowing hearts
And warming souls,
Or will love end?
A luminous fire
Seems embers in coals.

So can love be defined?
The breathtaking feeling,
The cooling mind,
The dangerous game that's hard to find,
A boundless agony;
That's love defined.

Arielle E. Williams
Williamstown, NJ

Dreaded Cancer

We often ask why we get the dreaded cancer
But so far, we haven't received the answer
The young, the old, children, husbands, and wives
Can never tell what will come in their lives
It seems that the good has to get sick
And at times, they die very quick
Others have to suffer, then suffer again
And there is no end to their pain
Some are so precious and pure
Just hoping they find the cure
In the hospitals in the children's ward
Those sweet little ones have it so hard
One great day when the golden bell will ring
There will be so many children to sing
Then their pain will be no more
Just sharing with Jesus on Heaven's shore
One day, Jesus will return and then
A thousand years and all cancer will end
And someday we will get the answer
Why so many had to get cancer

Dewey W. Craver
Winter Haven, FL

Set Them Free

When you find yourself trapped,
and out of fight,
when you lie awake
and can't sleep at night.
When your head says yes,
but your heart says no,
when you love someone
and can't let them go.
When things were good,
but they turn to bad,
when the person you love
just makes you sad.
When you feel like a prisoner
to the one you love,
when things come down
to push and shove.
When you feel like you're suffocating,
and there is no way out,
but you won't give up
through all the doubt.
When you love someone,
but it's just not right,
when all you do is
scream and fight.
When you love someone
and empty is all you will ever be,
you must be strong, and set them free.

Amanda L. King
St. Cloud, FL

Sometimes love and pain go hand in hand. As much as we may love someone, there
comes a time when the pain they cause is too much to bear, and we must let go of
that love. When we set them free, we are also set free. I am thankful for both love
and pain, for they have both set me free.

Let's Work It Out

Blood is flowing from my heart.
I don't want for us to part.
Pain is flowing from my brain.
I feel like I could go insane.
Tears are flowing from my eyes.
I hope it's not time for our goodbyes.

Don't you also feel the pain?
I thought we both felt the same.
Aren't your eyes filled with tears?
We've been together so many years.
This also must be hard for you
Remembering the day we said, "I do."

Let's try to work this out together,
Work hard and make our life much better.
Let's begin fresh from the start
To build a marriage that won't fall apart.
I'm willing to try if you are too.
I know you love me and I love you.

Sally A. Clelan
Clarence, NY

God's Gift of Love

God sent us the raindrops
That fall on our heads
Snowflakes
Falling to the ground

His patience, His love
Enough to go around
In Heaven
He is looking down

Don't give up
Stand straight, stand tall
God loves us one
He loves us all

Through hurdles of life
There may be many
Hold your head high
Look to the sky

Sun will shine
Bright as can be
God's love is brighter
Than you can see

How much love
He has for thee
Then we can turn to Him
And be glad

Mary L. Barbato
Lodi, OH

The Earth As I Once Knew It

There once was a green Earth I knew,
Now everything is thrown askew.
The lush jade grass is in the past,
All my memories are now ash.
Every lake of azure blue
In those pictures that I drew,
Yet the land that I knew
Unfortunately did not pull through.

Heaps of trash sit on the ground
Ten times higher than an a baseball mound.
Take the time, don't do a crime,
Please everyone, recycle.

Danielle M. Flood
Marlboro, NJ

I wrote this poem to increase environmental awareness and to show people how important it is to recycle. We only have one Earth and it's everyone's responsibility to preserve its beauty. I'd like to thank my family members and friends for convincing me to have my poem printed.

A Grader Day

There's a tale I'll relate to you,
It may sound crazy, but it's true.
Been grading roads for awhile,
Standing up was my style.
To a job, I'm on my way,
Doing twenty, I would say.
Doors, both open, a fine breeze.
All at once, I had to sneeze.
Chompers out, I don't know why,
Out the door they did fly.
Stopped the grader, went to fetch 'em,
In many pieces the tires had left them.
To the dentist after work,
He was amazed, he took a look.
Took the pieces and did repair,
Went to get them, be beware.
Picked them up, thank the Lord.
Put in my mouth, oh, my God!
Finally had new dentures made,
A foolish stunt, big bucks were paid.
One thing I learned, for that I swore,
Sit on the seat and close the door!

Wayne Hansen
Parsonsfield, ME

Six Feet

People say I slit my wrist
'Cause I wanted to die
But really when you broke my heart
You were the one who took hold of the knife
You cut me so deep
And it made me bleed
You were the one who dug my grave
Exactly six feet!

Dusti R. Noland
Fleming, OH

I'll Always Be Here

I just wanted to sit down and cry
I thought there was no more reason to try
It seemed as though all hope was gone
It seemed as though the devil had won
I knew that my God had the power
But in the midst of my darkest hour
In my greatest time of need
It felt like He'd forgotten me
But then I heard a still small whisper
It was the voice of my Savior
He said, "Child, there's no need to fear
For though you won't always feel me
I'll always be here."

Deborah A. Pierce
Knob Lick, KY

Brown Baby

Most adorable, alert bright shiny eyes
I ever seen.
Full of smiles, those chunky little legs moving.
Arms reaching out as though one to pick you up.
Smelling so fresh, sweet hair soft as cotton.
Baby so quiet, there's not any tears.
Moments seeing him with his mom.
Observing him, those smiles,
the brightest eyes I can recall.
I smile, baby smiles,
reaching little fingers moving.
Brown baby God's blessings.
All most precious in God's sight.
Brown baby!

Addy Cox
Newark, NJ

Give Me a Chance

Why do you want to kill me?
You don't even know me,
I haven't been born yet.
I could be a king or a pauper,
A male or a female.
One thing I know I am
Is a present
To you from God.
Give me a chance.

Peggy A. Mathiasen
Trenton, NJ

Don't Worry

Don't worry what you think you can change,
It's God who can and will your heart rearrange.
Why are you worrying about food, clothes, and shelter,
For God made the heavens and Earth, truly our helper.
When you're left helpless, sick in body you feel,
It was Christ; with His stripes, we are healed.
So don't worry about life's problems day after day,
He's our Deliverer, Protector, and guides us always,
For He promises to be with us forever and evermore.
To Him, we should love, praise, worship, and adore,
For Christ is the ruler of this world, come what may.
Don't worry what Man may think or say,
Just keep His love in your heart to stay.

Joan Y. Scott
The Villages, FL

Expression of Love

I can feel your heartbeat
when you're next to me.
It's as special as a present
under the Christmas tree.
Having you to love me
means the world to me.
I love when you hold me
in your arms so tenderly.
With you by my side,
and you in my heart,
I know for sure
we will never part.
I know I love you,
and you love me.
I know now our love
was meant to be.

Catherine I. Heckman
Farmingdale, NY

1996

Laughter, joy, health, and love
That truly was unimaginable
For this time in his life
I bore all this wonderful being
To share all he had and all he didn't
Life, family, and friends meant the
World to him and he deserved it all

A last minute of "I love you, son"
"I love you, Mom"
Never to know it would be the last
The last of all I loved
Always to roam in my life with
Questions of how could this be
In a heart that can never, ever explain

To hold on to memories
That hurt to remember
But they are all I have
With pictures that smile
He smiles and says
"Mom, I'll always be with you"

Guillermina Walker
Bronx, NY

God's Light

Thinking of a child so young and innocent
You wonder what their life will be
Where their life will lead
Will they grow into a fine person
Give when someone's in need
Little face so gentle and sweet
Little eyes what will they see
Will they see God's light
Where will their dreams take them
Will they carry them to the highest mountaintop
Little ears what will they hear
Will they hear sounds of music
Will their soul be filled with love
Looking at their little hands
Will they grow strong
Clasp their hands in prayer
What path will they take
Along life's journey
Will they grow into someone whom you can depend
To whom you can be proud
Will this child give you hope joy and love
Or give you tears
Will the sun shine on a rainy day
Or the clouds fade away

Laura Jean M. Barbato
Lodi, OH

Dare to Love

You slipped into my dreams a long time ago,
the first time it happened, I just don't know.
The more I am around you, the more clear it becomes
there's just something about you;
my attention, you have won.
I think about you all the time,
I try to think of you as a friend,
but sometimes in my sweetest dreams,
that's not the way it ends.
I am a married woman, this I don't deny,
but with all the feelings I feel for you,
my heart is in a bind.
I'm longing to be with you in every single way,
to hold you, to touch you to feel you;
one look in your eyes and I melt away.
I can't talk to anyone about the way I feel,
so I write it down on paper, that's my only appeal.
But sometimes when I think about you, I wonder if you might
have any feelings for me, or is it just my fight?
I can't help the way I feel about you,
I didn't want it to start,
but if you ever dare to love me, I have the key to your heart.

Shirley A. Judson
Jefferson, GA

Flying

Flying high in the sky.
Soaring, roaring and smooth flowing.
My, this airplane is really going!
Soon, time to land and
I can't wait to feel the sand.
Sand under my feet
is oh, so neat
at the beach.
The beach is a sweet
treat for the body and soul.
This plane did not land
fast enough, 'cause we
are still flying,
flying high in the sky. . . .

Gloria J. Roberson
Rochdale, NY

Sleeping with a Bear

Have you ever dreamed here and there,
What it must be like sleeping with a bear?

All that fur and a big flat nose.
Big feet and ears too, I suppose.

Another thing most people will dread,
How does a bear fit into my little bed?

Cold winter nights, a bear would keep you warm,
Nestled in all that fur, away from the storm.

Out there are some things that bears do wrong,
They sleep and snore all winter long.

I would like a bear all fuzzy and clean,
A friendly bear, not one that is mean.

I'm lucky as lucky can be,
Because I have a bear who sleeps with me.

He is not too big, doesn't take up much space,
Quite cute, you know, with a friendly face.

So at day's end, I climb the stair
To my little bed to sleep with my teddy bear.

Paul E. Schwarze
Clinton Corners, NY

Winter Fairyland

My winter "fairyland" is here.
Oh, yes, you'd like to know
how things like that seem to appear in April without snow!
The sun came bursting forth at 6:00,
and there before my eyes were jeweled trees,
and sparkling chains draped just below the skies.
All winter I kept waiting to see this grand disguise,
but when the spring winds from the south brought budding—
no surprise!
And there has been no sleet to spawn this winter paradise,
I just accepted this to be a year without my prize!
When I was young, oh, such a thrill
to wander down our lane
after a storm of raging sleet and slashing, freezing rain,
then touch the cool and sparkling jewels
a-dancing in the sun, and skate along the Cinder Drive
because the sleet had come!
Oh, these are fascinating gems
dropped there, for God in love
gives us these thrills to lift us up
until we go above!

Avis M. Morford-Hawkins
Greenfield, IN

Our faith in the living God and His Son, Jesus Christ, will carry us through this twenty-first century. January 21, 1924, my parents, Ola Chesterfield and Leona Clark Apple, were entertaining the folk gathered for the Mays, Indiana, Farm Bureau. They sang and played piano, violin, guitar, and French harp. As the program ended, my mother told her daddy, George Butler McClellan Clark, to go home and tell Mommy to put the water on the heat. At 1:00 a.m., Avis Marie Apple was welcomed into the big farmhouse. Since crying, I've been singing, playing piano, cello, bells, and organ; also writing poetry, newspaper articles, and Christian literature ever since. Eighty-six years and three husbands later, I'm still playing instruments for church.

School's Out

Silence roars through empty halls,
Bouncing off walls,
Slithering under doors,
Wending its way through legs
Of abandoned desks
Of learning.

Empty chambers;
Forlorn echelons where whispers
Of long-forgotten facts resound.
Curled-edged posters
Of faraway places and times
Hang askew on scuffed-up walls.

White-coated erasers
Lie inert beside worn stubs of chalk.
Empty blackboards, dust-shrouded and plain,
Divested of words once used to open minds,
To activate that innate human quest
For knowledge.

Mary J. Little
Morehead, KY

Consider

If Jesus were a Black man,
would He still your Savior be,
or would you turn the other way
and say, "He's not for me"?

Would you just smile politely
when you saw Him face to face,
but murmur low within your heart,
"I care not for Your grace"?

Would the color of His skin
stir up anger, doubt, or fear,
and would you feel resentment rise
when you saw Him come near?

If Jesus were a Black man,
what would your answer be?
Well, don't tell me, just tell the Lord
as you fall upon your knee!

Mary B. Williams
Utica, OH

The Memory Quilt

Grandma sat there solemnly, quilt on her knees
Every piece sewn with love, every stitch agrees
In her hand there's a locket, half-open, half-closed
She puts it back in her pocket, her countenance aglow
Could it be thoughts of precious days gone by
A buggy ride in the country, or hot pumpkin pie
Maybe a hug, kind word, a kiss on the cheek
A childhood memory, or loved one she seeks
With tear-filled eyes, takes it out once more
Then to the task at hand, just as before
She's tired and worn, but perseveres on
The memory quilt finished as the sun greets the dawn
A smile creeps over her face, like a warm gentle breeze
Staring out the window at the falling leaves
She settles back in the rocker, composed
In her hand there's a locket, half-open, half-closed

Michael R. Meadows
Owingsville, KY

To Unknown Poets

To the ones we miss in the midst of all the confusion

One never knows what life will bring when life is so short.
In the emptiness of all lives, but there's more;
the mist goes away, it was all an illusion.
The life that we lived was the conclusion.

Brian D. Vaslet
Pawtucket, RI

Untitled

I sit here in my favorite chair,
the weather is cold, the trees are bare.
I love my family, friends, and life,
as seasons march on with drum and fife.
The snow will come with winds that blow,
it's hard to remember the grasses that grow.
All the yards all covered in white,
memories come back of a long-ago night.
My mind drifts back as I sit inside
of parents, hot chocolate, and sleds that glide.
There was a barrel with wood, fire and smoke,
though I felt cold when I first awoke.

Eleanor M. Prigmore
Seward, PA

The Journey

I'm about to debark on a journey
A journey I must take alone.
I hope these long narrow highways
Somehow will lead me to home.

I leave all my loved ones behind me,
My wife and my children so dear.
They must all know that I love them,
For each one, I'm shedding a tear.

I sense the darkness around me,
And I fear my journey is done—
But wait, there's a light in the darkness
And someone is calling me home.

I'll wait here for my loved ones
As they pass through the valley below.
Hand in hand, we will climb up the mountain
Till we reach the highest plateau.

Now that my journey is over,
A new time has already begun.
We'll bask in the love of our Savior,
For you know, He's God's only Son.

Dean G. Thomas
Liverpool, NY

On Him You Can Depend

Sometimes things seem impossible
and I really would like to run away,
but God seems to always strengthen me
and gives me the courage to stay.
I have to learn to trust in God, because
there really is and never will be anyone else.
The only person that can harm me is me, myself, and I,
but that will never happen if on the Lord I rely.
I'm sometimes up and sometimes down and often in between,
but the times I am down and feeling low,
I have my God on whom to lean.
If I have but one life to live and one time to live it right,
I would love to think I gave it my all
and did not quit without a good fight.
When things seem impossible and hard for me to understand,
I can close my eyes and pray to God
because He is more than just a mere man.
So when you are feeling down and out
and there is no where to turn,
just take a second and humble yourself
and give the Lord your utmost concerns.
He will take care of them for you,
and that is without a doubt,
all you need do is talk to Him;
He already knows what it is all about.
On Him you can depend.

Constance Mims
Syracuse, NY

Our Children

They're here today and gone tomorrow.
They bring you joy and sometimes sorrow.
Now heed this warning note from me,
And enjoy then while you have them, see.
The tiny babe, all bundled warm,
You must love and shield from harm,
And bathe and feed and cuddle tight
And sometimes be kept awake at night.
The toddler is a funny sight,
The things he gets into are a fright.
My drawer, shortening, soap, and sure,
He samples them all and looks for more.
The school child, oh, how can it be
That he can stay away from me.
And I his talk will surely miss,
But yes, it must need come to this.
First, second, third grade and four,
And now he is nearing graduation's door.
He's found another friend to take
My place, and this too I must face.
He's gone now, and someday I'll see
A little babe like he used to be.
I'll cuddle it and sigh a strain
And wish it could be him again.

Mildred Eifler
Marietta, OH

All the Single Mothers

My heart goes out to single mothers,
Your dedication, patience, and time.
My heart cries out for single mothers.
At times you can't clear your mind.
The father is gone,
But you're not alone.
Look to a higher power above,
He can help you be strong.
The child begins to wonder,
Where is Daddy? Is he coming back?
As you sit and ponder
How to tell them that a father is what they'll lack.
You need money,
"Friends" are acting funny.
Look to a higher power above,
He can make dark skies sunny.
Where is the help when you need it most,
Diapers, wipes, clothes?
Suffering from lack of sleep and post-traumatic stress.
Where is the father? Nobody knows.
My heart goes out to single mothers,
Your diligence, kind heart, and endurance.
My heart cries out for single mothers.
In the end, this will pay off
When you can collect his insurance money!

Andrea L. Oglesby
Seneca, SC

Christmastime

Christmastime is almost here,
A time the children hold ever so dear.

The snow is beginning to fall
Upon the buildings large and small.

Bells are ringing,
All the carolers are singing.

A dog darts across the street,
His master he runs to meet.

Santa will soon be making his way across the sky
With a twinkle in his eye.

Lots of toys fill his sled
For Makayla, Susie, Camron, and baby Ned.

Christmastime is almost here,
A time the children hold ever so dear.

Wanda C. Burdette
Anderson, SC

Color Thief

The funeral flowers came
To center the painting of grief.
The surroundings were brown and gray,
The colors provided relief.
Though vibrant and gray are not the same,
The palette mixed into just one name
As death became all colors' thief.

Judith W. Lynch
Waldwick, NJ

Under Construction

I'm under construction, don't tear me down.
Build me up so I can stay around,
Not going to complain of what I been through.
Thank God for His Word that will see me through.
I'm under construction, my body has been broken and bruised.
What can you do to heal my wounds?
I'll call on His name, who is that?
Jesus Christ He'll heal you like that.
I'm under construction,
Satan don't care,
What trouble you're in, he'll keep you there.
Satan the destroyer can't see you.
He doesn't want you to get closer to Thee.

Linda Henley
Richmond, VA

Happy Birthday

I wish you joy on your birthday
In a very special way,
Although, of course, your happiness,
I wish for every day.

On your birthday, the world seems
Somehow to start anew,
And I would wish all joys of life
Right now would come to you.

Birthdays come like springtime,
When the Earth is bright and gay,
And I would wish for all your life
Would follow in that way.

So may this birthday morning
Proclaim for you a new start
That will bring life's greatest blessing
Is the wish that's in my heart.

Kathleen Bates
Moundville, AL

This poem, "Happy Birthday," I dedicate to a special lady, Lois E. Harris, in honor of her ninety-third birthday. I have been one of her caregivers for over three years, and during this time, I have grown to love her dearly. Miss Lois, "LoLo" is an amazing woman with a beautiful spirit, and I admire her devotion to her Lord, family, and friends. She is a wonderful role model, and I will forever treasure her love and friendship.

Heaven

I looked at the sky and it was blue.
As I looked toward Heaven, I said Lord, I love You!
My sixteen-year-old grandson came to live with You
and put us all in a stew.
I know he is having so much fun,
he doesn't know what to do.
He was always so happy and thinking
fun things for you.
We miss him so much and I bet
he misses us too.
I will be so happy when we will be
together again!
The tears will stop and the laughter will roll,
we will forget we have gotten old.
Keep smiling, Devan, God knows best,
He sometimes puts us through a rigid test.

Wilma S. Thomason
Good Hope, GA

love's a blur

all the chaos, all the confusion
life is short, but we are hardly a-movin'

strands of time moving quickly with force
crossing the section, unaware of the course

lots of joys, lots of sorrows
with thoughts of our desolate tomorrows

with ideas of hope inspires fear
as slick as it begins to draw near

all the love, all the hate
are you my one and only, my soul mate?

put my soft hand in yours
to see our bond beyond the wars

lots of silence, lots of tears
how long is eternity, how many years?

a bottle of liquor in my hand
on the beach, alone in the sand

all our dreams and all our choices
why can't you hear me over all the voices?

dreaming my dreams would forever come true
what can one do when i'm still in love with you!

Kristen M. Bertolacci
Coral Springs, FL

Mother and Dad

You gave me life,
You gave me love,
You gave me happiness.
I gave you pain and joy.
You watched me grow
You watched me stray,
You watched me, a wife-to-be.
You watched a grandson unfold.
You nourished a cocoon and found a butterfly.
Your butterfly touched this Earth
For just a little while,
Flitting here and flitting there
A resting place to find.
A haven she found,
A full blown rose and a bud.
She nourished them for a while
And it was time to go.
Peace and serenity was her goal.
She turned her wings upward
Into the night,
Until she became a star
That twinkles every night.

Norma N. Alliston
Ypsilanti, MI

399

Destiny

Green grass growing beneath my feet
Peaceful thoughts as I go to sleep
As I lay in my bed and hear a grasshopper sing
Joy to my heart these sounds bring
Birds all chirping as I begin my day
These are wonderful things to you I say
A deer grazing in the pasture in the distance
As a squirrel climbs a tree with the utmost persistence
Mother Nature has granted us such gifts
And to my soul she shall uplift
What a feeling to watch so close at hand
But all shall be ruined it's the destiny of Man
To kill and murder only the strong survive
But not as long as I am alive
To ruin this planet and all of her splendors
Once it's all gone there's no room to mend her
But maybe it's just the destiny of Man
To live life the best he can
And if this shall mean to ruin all that is dear
When Mother Nature calls we shall all fear
The reign of terror she will inflict
And all of Man shall live to regret
The great ruin in which we have caused
And we shall see in the end all of our flaws.

James C. DeVaughn
Freedom, PA

My Life

My name is Sarah,
but this isn't my life.
Who is this man
calling me wife?

I have a daughter?
How can this be?
I'm a child myself,
but she does look like me.

I'm a college student?
No, that's not me.
I dropped out of high school.
I went to court for truancy.

Then I realize
how much time has passed.
This is my present life
and that was my past.

I'm no longer a little girl,
nor am I a child,
so I kiss my daughter, light a cigarette,
then sit back and smile.

Sarah J. Sutton
Berlin Heights, OH

God Bless America

We Americans have much strength and pride
And as Americans, we have nothing to hide.
Forced busing our children is not an American way,
For that means us parents have nothing to say.
Dictators use force, not Americans; we are free.
Legislators pass these laws, not you and me,
Forced busing contributes to polluting the air,
It seems that our lawmakers don't seem to care.
Our children are in danger every single day,
They could be hurt or missing, who are we to say?
Busing causes traffic jams in each and every city,
We pay for the fuel consumed, oh, what a pity.
The cost for busing our children, we cry,
Should be used for a better education, that's not lie.
Compared to other countries, we well know
Our educational system is far below.
Lawmakers, for us Americans, the time has come
Look in your hearts is the appeal of everyone.
It is time that our voices should be heard,
So lawmakers, carefully read every word.
It's the home of the brave and the land of the free.
Please stop dictating to us, give back our liberty.

George S. Valenti
East Boston, MA

Feed Me!

I was sitting on the counter
Beside a box of kibble
When I had the sudden urge
To have a little nibble.
My human was reading her newspaper.
I thought, "I must get her out of her seat.
I need to get her attention
And get her on her feet."
So I strolled over to the paper towels
And pawed, then pawed some more,
Until the roll was half unwound
And the towels were on the floor.
My human jumped up and yelled at me.
"Stop, stop right now!"
I told her in my catlike way,
"I want to have some chow."
She re-rolled the paper towels,
She was in a stew!
She thinks I am demanding,
And yes, I guess that's true!
After my snack I apologized
For my tendency to irk.
Secretly, though, I was thinking,
"Her response time needs some work!"

Ann C. Zepke
Fort Wayne, IN

Quest for Guardian Angel

Oh, Lord
Hear thou my quest for a guardian angel
My hair is turning grey
Joints in my body, they all ache
Hoping, skipping, running, jumping
Was a piece of cake

Oh, Lord
Hear thou my quest for a guardian angel
To help me do all the things I used to do
To help my life remake
To a dream of a pseudo piece of cake

Oh, Lord
With no guardian angel
This life will never remake
This life will just go on living
But life will nevermore be a piece of cake

Oh, Lord
Send me a guardian angel
May it be someday?
I pray and pray and pray

Philip Pavda
Voorhees, NJ

My parents were Russian immigrants. They met on a boat sailing to America.
When they arrived in America, they studied English and earned American citizens
certificates. They were married, and I was born. While growing up, I experienced
the shock of losing both my parents to incurable cancer. A friend helped me live
through my grief to such a high degree that I nicknamed him "my guardian angel."
Thereby, I was inspired to write my poem, "Quest for Guardian Angel."

Winter

The trees are desolate once more, and the leaves have
fallen to blanket the earth.
During the day, it is so frigid that humans can see their
breath and there is a chance for storms.
At times, you can hear the silence of the night because
who wants to gamble with the lower temperature?
People for years have enjoyed having snowball fights, making
snowmen and other animals of milky snow, and some even like to
shovel it.
People and their families like to escape for the weekend
to ski resorts for many reasons.
Some like the mountain air filled with snow and cold.
It is a time for families to bond by the fire with hot cocoa.
Some people also ski down the slopes, feeling the rush of wind
around them, but others are watching out for the treacherous trees.
There are even some "crazy" men and women who think it is a great
idea to go swimming in thirty-degree weather and colder.
During these months, the light of day turns into night that much
sooner and precipitation from the gentle blanketing of powder
to a dreadful blizzard.
I just like the smell of embers of wood ablaze in the air
of day and night as I walk collecting my thoughts,
even the temperature of winter, and yes, I like to shovel snow.
If the weatherman can predict the weather right, then we might
know how much wood is needed for the winter months.
Some people hate this season for the delays
and the coldness it brings, but some people value this time of year
because for many, it brings out the kid in us all.

Matthew Amer
Massapequa, N

Dark Child

The ball suspended in air
Just couldn't catch it
Just didn't care
Tears hangin' around
Droppin' down
Takin' fun away
Dark child
If only I could have laughed more
I was cured for a while
Only with a smile
If only I could have been more of a child
Somehow I missed the fun
Somehow I missed the rays of the sun
I missed the day
Play by play
And before I knew it
I had the weight of world
On my shoulders

Veronica Blackman
Southfield, MI

A Poem for the President

Dear Mr. President, during these hard times,
Here are some thoughts that are on all of our minds!
There is the war in Iraq, have we really won?
Day after day, it seems only to have begun.
There is an issue of prayer in school.
Isn't it still an answer and a strong tool?
Health care, insurance, and medicines are out of sight.
Just going to the pharmacy is a real fright!
Gasoline prices are sure not funny.
Why to drive our vehicles must it cost so much money?
Unemployment lines are long, paychecks too low!
In which direction can a poor person go?
Same sex marriages? To me, such a disgrace!
As far as a family picture, for them there is no place.
In my Bible it does mention Adam is for Eve.
Nowhere do I see Adam and Steve!
Mr. President, we know you are one of the best.
Over and over, you have been put to the test!
You are in our prayers, our hopes are still on you
With God in the picture, He will always pull us through.

Marion J. Fowler
Jacksonville, FL

America, the Red, the White, the Blue

So many have given their all, that red, the blood, it's true.
They've paid the ultimate price, gave up their lives for me and you.
Without a moment's hesitation,
many have died to bless this great nation.
The red is the symbol of the blood, it's always a part of our banner to
remind us of those courageous men of honor
who fought for our freedom to keep us full of pride and truth.
So white those navy uniforms, those coverings of purity and truth.
Never given in defeat. The white is there, so clean.
Standing tall and straight the ships of valor as they head towards the
perils of the seas, then launch those guns of strength
when enemies seek to harm the quest of freedom.
The white is the purity of freedom, preserved by the blood.
So let us salute those coats of arms, the sailors of the waters
as blue as the sky of the Earth, the blue of the flying air force
so magnificently defends our way of life.
The blue of Old Glory always shines right through.
When the cloud of evil threaten freedom of the world,
those jets soar with the wings of conviction
as they blaze trails of spirit across the sky.
America, so blessed, and so true,
God blessed this land for me and you,
but it's defended by the red, the white, and the blue.
The army, the navy, the marines, the air force, the reserves,
the Coast Guard, the local police, the firemen all so true!
They defend our way of life, they give each day for you!
God bless America! America, the red, the white, the blue!

Terry A. Reece
Detroit, MI

A Man Called Dick

Long ago there was a man called Dick
He learned to live with a walking stick
He might lift up your dress and cause quite a mess
Long ago there was a man called Dick

Then there was a man name called Dick
Who had to use more than one stick
It wasn't that fun but he got it done
Then there was a man called Dick

Later there was a man called Dick
He motored along on a scooter
That would get him there sooner
Later there was a man called Dick

Finally there was a man named Dick
God took him away because he was sick
Now he is at peace
His suffering did cease
He doesn't need a stick or a scooter
He's walking much smoother
This man that was called Dick

Josephine H. Adams
Dexter, NY

Winter Snow

Snow is falling, what a wonderful sight.
It glows and sparkles in the sunlight.
The children are riding on sleds in the snow,
Laughing and giggling as they go to and fro.

Making a snowman with a carrot nose,
Using stones for the eyes that never close.
Branches for arms and pebbles for the mouth.
When they're all done, the children will shout.

One thing more for the snowman they made,
A scarf to keep him warm and a hat for the shade.
The sun has gone down, no more time to play.
They will be out tomorrow to start a new day.

Carmella F. Smith
Chicopee, MA

About Me

It must be about me,
Don't you see?
Or it's all about others
And how they see me
Family and friends,
They laugh and play,
But don't you see?
I must have the last say.
Anecdotes and events
That you want to share,
If they are not about me,
Why should I care?
Going through life without
Sisters or brothers taught me
That caring is not about others.
Now that I have spoken,
I hope you will see.
If it is all about anything,
It must be all about me.

Jonathan D. Goldstein
Dix Hills, NY

The Incan City

How could I forget
My city on the hill
Where God and Man conspire
To awe the sight and steal the breath

Where God with care has pinched the earth
And made it into glorious mounds
And sprinkled green and petall'd life
And streaked His colors 'cross the stone

Where Man carves ridges in the rock
And builds his stone on top of stone
Whispering in the light of day
Of ancient fears and ancient dreams
Casting shadows in the folds

Where music rises in the air
The song of whittled flutes
Dancing on the wind
Calling back, calling back
A time before the pale men came

Grace V. Hitchman
Cherry Hill, NJ

Falling Leaves

There's a tinge of fall in the air today
amid colored leaves all ablaze,
red, yellow, and rustic brown.
The autumn leaves come tumbling down;
a deep red mahogany sunset glows,
just like the autumn leaves' shades of gold.
In autumn's frosty sky,
the colorful leaves start to fly.
Across flocks of geese in V-formation
in joyous celebration
of fall's rainbow colors, autumn gold jubilation.

Soaring colored leaves fly way up high,
like birds on the wing in the sky.
The hilltops, thick with color, tell the story
of beautiful autumn in all its glory.
The gypsy leaves come tumbling down
in shades of amber, red, and brown.

Minnie L. Burns
Carnesville, GA

Demonically Divine

She walks like a goddess
her toes curling through the sand
With strides so graceful
she'll make the knees buckle on a man
Her breasts high and firm
she stands tall and thin
With a dazzling beauty so divine
I couldn't help but get sucked in—
sucked into her eyes,
and her thick, salacious thighs
If only I could've seen
all of her wickedness and lies
for when she saw my face
she smiled and offered me her hand
dragging me through fire and broken glass
making a mockery of a man
In the beginning, it was love,
I felt happy, I felt whole
Little did I know with every kiss,
she was inhaling my heart and soul
Once she had my heart,
she continued on her way
She added the broken pieces to her collection,
and she holds them till this day.

Allan P. O'Brien
Plattsburgh, NY

For the Students of Virginia Tech

Did you just wake up yesterday
With killing on your mind?
Did you have your victims chosen or
Shoot the first that you could find?
Did you stop and think of the mother
That would be left without her son?
Did you stop and think of your own parents
Before you turned and picked up your gun?
Did you feel any compassion
When you shut their eyes for good?
Did you try to blame somebody else
As if you really could?
Did you even stop to ask yourself
Why you were killing so many, so fast?
Did you want the terror to go on and on
Until you shot your last?
And when you met your Maker
Did you bow down and say
Did you see the fear of the students
The thirty-two I killed today?
Did you expect to be forgiven
For their deaths and all the pain?
Can you tell me anything at all
About what you had hoped to gain?

Alpha B. Campbell
Leland, NC

Words

The potential within each soul is endless
But must be nurtured in the proper way
With love and understanding
Being poured out every day.
The self-image of each person
Must be formed with tender care
For we are very fragile
And respond to what we hear.
So let the words of our mouth be pleasing—
For they are powerful things.
They create in us vast feelings.
They can make the heart have wings.
But they can also cause great pain and hurt and fear.
They can destroy a tender heart by being unaware
Of all the needs within the core
Of each eternal soul.
Yes, words can wound or even kill
Or heal and make one whole.

Joyce H. Wolf
Shoreham, NY

September 11

I stand in radiant splendor
Amongst celestial spheres
Awakened to a higher left
Beyond my tender mortal years

I stretch forth both my hands
One to you who grieve my loss
The other touches God
My soul becomes a cross

There is no death but only life
The love and light we each adore
As I am first to make this passage
Glimpse through me an open door

Where hierarchies of light are weaving
Angelic forces to all life streams
Bathed in beauty and in glory
Beyond temporal thoughts and dreams

As we were linked upon Earth's plane
So also here our voices may be heard
For was commune in thoughts of love
Once more united in God's holy Word

William Stansmore
Sunderland, MA

Love

Can we go back to the '80s for one sweet day?
We can make unforgettable moments.
I can't live without you.
I can't imagine being without the sweet look
In your eyes. I want to say, "I love you" to you
For the rest of my life.
We're headed for something strong for years
To come.

The sound of my heart starts beating
When I hear you say those sweet words, "I love you."
The sound of my heart starts beating
When I hear you say those sweet words, "I do."
The sound of my heart starts beating when I
Hear you say those sweet words, "I promise
I'll be by your side from this day on."

Our love is the power that holds us together.
I want to love you until the day I die,
And when my day comes to pass,
I'll wait for you in Heaven.

Ashley L. See
Harpers Ferry, WV

A Glimpse

Imagine all flowers blooming at the same time
Symphony of technicolor
Joyously fine

What if all humans were freed of their pain
Finally the realness
Truthfully insane

Nothing could be bartered or bought with money
Curiously provocative
Practically funny

Every being caressed and coddled the same
Meticulously incubated
Disregarding position or fame

Time to reflect, meditate, and pray
Defending humbly
Choosing reentry or to stay

An environment of conscience love
Blissful awareness
Could it be a glimpse of the above?

Felicia Frestan
Bronx, NY

Mr. Obama—a Presidential Tribute

He stood at the top of the steps;
Looking down, his thoughts were mixed.
He had been elected president
Of the most powerful country
In the world.
Did he deserve it? He thought so.
He had studied and worked hard
To reach his goal.

He was not a fool.
He remembered his family and
Friends who had cheered and
Encouraged him.
He looked down at the crowd below.
He must not let them down.
He was not a fool.
He knew he had enemies who
Wished to destroy his image.
Many knew they might not achieve
Such a lofty position. Few did.
His face had an enigmatic smile
As he descended the steps.

He was not a fool.
The people who were plotting
To destroy him were fools.

Frances L. Wilson
Wheeling, WV

The New Flower of Maherally (Simple Heart)

For my Ukrainian bride, Renata

Water lilies clean as fresh from springs as a drink so deep.
No reason to stay,
But my eye still weeps.

In my book of poem and rhyme,
Living in love within God and the changing of His times.

Come now to me quick,
I will pay so fair.
The trees in winter become so bare.

In the springtime, my sentimental heart
With tears that fell from my eye,
My water lilies cannot be destroyed, wither, or die.

I never turned my back to you in such troubled times.
Renata, travel and stay with me,
My gift for you is in my rhyme.

Anthony A. Kosak
Palm Harbor, FL

What If?

What if we took a trip and had more
Fun than we thought we would?
What if we flew to Miami if we could?
What if you spent the holidays with
Me and always made me laugh,
Baked me a treat and we split half and half?
What if we slept near each other and dreamt
Of us all night?
What if you are the one and we never fight?
What if we love each other with all our hearts,
What if we tried out for a play and got the leading parts?
What if our love was so strong, the passion so intense?
I can feel it build up the long-lasting suspense.
What if we traveled all over the world?
What if you held me and my lips curled?
What if we have the best cars?
What if we fell in love under the stars?
I could go on and on forever,
Always a "What if?" in my mind.
I just hope you are my one of a kind.

Felishia-Jean V. Pereira
New Bedford, MA

A Cancer Journey

Cancer is a terrible disease,
it definitely does not put anyone at ease.
With doctor appointments and hospital visits galore,
sometimes there is no way of knowing what is in store.

When hopes are down and bring you astray,
the best thing to do is to pray.
In fact, faith is the key,
we are like branches off God's tree.

Our personal angels are blessings in disguise,
they are God's love, peace, and prize.
Seek out your friends who care the most,
they are there to lean on like a post.

This illness brings us down various directions,
but we must stay focused on Christ's resurrection.
When the going gets tough,
turn to God and He'll lead you out of the rough.

My mom is a survivor and an inspiration to all,
please keep the faith, be strong and always stand tall.
Although life gets crazy, we need to love,
spread the good news and be God's dove.

Happy Easter to all!

Alysse T. Teixeira
Ludlow, MA

The World's Greatest Gift

Christmas to me is a time of joy,
Joy in the hearts of every girl and boy,
Not because of the gift we receive
But because of a Savior in whom we believe.
The world is so full of flesh and lust,
Anything ahead of Jesus seems to be a must.
People running rampant here and there,
Trying to find the right gift to show they care.
They miss the greatest gift in the entire world
Hunting the perfect one for some boy or girl.
Wouldn't it be wonderful if they'd remember that tiny stall
Where the greatest of miracles happened for all!
Ah! What a night this must have been
As a light shone about and a star led the men.
"My, what a Savior!" should be our heart's cry
That Jesus came and loved us and then He would die.
Have you accepted this gift today?
Do you share His story as you go on your way?
It's the world's greatest gift, tell it again and again
How Jesus was born and lived among men.
So when Christmas passes and the lights grow dim,
Does your light still shine pointing others to Him?

Merle Bell
Cairo, GA

The Tomb

I lay on my back on top of the sod-covered root cellar,
which my family referred to as "the tomb,"
for that is what it looked like.
It seemed more fitting as a place for dead bodies
than as a place to store vegetables.
Long ago it had been converted into a garage for farm machinery.
It was a cool afternoon in the summer of my tenth year,
and I had absolutely nothing to do, or wanted to do
but lie on my back and stare up at the white, wispy clouds
racing across a bright blue sky.
My small yellow dog lay beside me,
content to rest peacefully with his doggy dreams.
High above us, the clouds took on different shapes,
sometimes looking like dogs or cats or cows.
Then they would change shapes and appear as buildings or trees.
My imagination would turn them into grotesque creatures
set on devouring other clouds of more benign shapes.
I would lie there for long periods of time,
quite happy in my youthful musings,
while I waited to be called to supper.

Gerry Davis
Epsom, NH

Pearls of My Life

Pearl is the sister I never had
And wished for all my life
Someone to share with and
Hold close to your heart
And dream you never would part

She appeared to me when I was three
And then again at ten
And through the years that pearl of my life
Appeared again and again

Now a pearl from the ocean is still a pearl
Although the size may vary
A pearl of your life comes with many names
Helen, Doris, or Mary

The size of the heart is always the same
In whatever form she appears
There is love and closeness and sharing of dreams
My pearls and a sister are one

Betty Laughlin
Calais, ME

Let It Be

You smile at me, you make my body quiver.
I see the twinkle in your eyes, you send me a shiver
Up my spine; a touch of your hand,
I hope you understand
I love you more than you know,
And that's why I gotta let you go.

Our love isn't the same, we've drifted apart,
But you'll always have a place in my heart.
Oh, baby, please, you've faded away,
I wanna be serious, you wanna play.

Don't make it hard, it doesn't feel right,
I'll think of you on those lonely nights.
You're always on my mind,
I think about you all the time.
It won't be long, just a break
To see if it was fake.
Our love, it seemed so real to me,
So just simply let it be.

Victoria L. Showalter
Baltimore, MD

Irish Beauty

Her beauty stopped me in my tracks
She stood there with a puzzled look
But a child she seemed to me when I left

My duty done, service over
Returning to family, home
Searching faces from my youth

Whoa, my car, my steed, halts to see this girl
Now stunning woman from my youth, my past
Standing there this red-haired Irish beauty

Capturing my eye unable to blink
As I remember now a time
Forty-five years ago

When I invited her
To coffee and later proposed
She said yes to both

Six years traveling round the world
Brought me back to find a love even now
Invigorating my heart

Perry L. Phipps
Severn, MD

Love Hurts

Roses are red,
violets are blue,
you are like a rose
that blooms in June
that smells so sweet
like honeydew.
That I would do anything
for my love, for you.
Being alone without you
is tearing me apart.
No one will ever take
your place in my life.
It will never be the same
with someone else.
It may be better or worse,
it's hard to tell
until it happens.

Dave W. Hutchison
Rochester, IN

One Man's Dream

On September 11, 2001
America woke to the brilliant sun
We did not know what would come our way
When four planes left on that fateful day
One man's dream was to kill a nation
By using its own to cause devastation
Where two buildings once stood erect
There's a gaping hole where we genuflect
When one plane flew into the Pentagon
We felt that all of our hope was gone
A field in Pennsylvania, once calm and serene
Had become the site of a horrific scene
That day, God claimed many a soul
As one of them yelled out, "Let's roll"
Where on this day, that man's dream ignited
The patriotic torch of a country united
And in the end, when he's through crying
He'll see that it's still Old Glory flying.

Judith A. Melvin
Blackwood, NJ

The Few, the Proud, the Marines

When the fatherland calls, I'm there,
Fighting, struggling against the beast,
The enemy which hates life,
The enemy which hates joy,
The enemy which hates America
Is an enemy of mine.

America, our mother,
What you desire us to do,
Your sons aren't going to let you alone,
We will be there to protect you.

No need for another army,
It is us you should seek.
Trust, believe we aren't weak.

Klajdi Plasari
Bronx, NY

The Rain

When I watch the rain coming down,
Each drop represents a tear
Of God over the sins of you and me
Each year after year.
He's crying over His creation,
And all the things He sees.
He did not mean it to be this way
When He died to set us free,
Yet the rain of tears keep pouring
To baptize us again and again,
And cleanse us from the stain of death
That could swallow us up in the end.
As you and I feel the rain,
We run for cover to escape.
Can you imagine how God must feel
When we turn from His faith?
Can you see a tear when children get shot,
And die for no good reason?
Can you hear the patter of a broken heart
As we go through different world seasons?
Rain a tear for the sick, homeless, and prison-bound,
Rain a tear for all.
Rain a tear because the end will come,
Just be ready for God when He calls.

Mary Sherman
Paterson, NJ

The Hawk

It seems, at first, kind of awful
To see such a thing from afar,
But I stay there, quietly, for a while.
To me, on second thought, that it was so extremely natural.
If I wanted to stop it,
I should have second thoughts
To stop this natural occurrence,
A hawk from killing its prey
That it has grasped in its claws.
It would be like trying to stop a rageful river,
One that is full, from the mountains' melted snow,
One that is free to run in the spring.
I could not stop such a natural thing,
This hawk from killing its prey.
Who am I to stop this hawk
From doing such a natural thing?

Brian A. Couture
Farmington, NH

I came up with the thought that put this poem together exiting a shot clinic at a mental health clinic in Dower, New Hampshire. I was diagnosed with schizophrenia many years ago, a couple years after I got out of military service. As I exited the building, I saw a hawk that had captured and was killing a pigeon. That's how "The Hawk" came about.

I Am Sorry I Am Weak

I am sorry I am weak
I wonder why you say such things
I hear the laughter and porch swings
I want to dance around and sing
I am sorry I am weak
I pretend to be so strong
I feel so alone
I touch the rain, this seems all wrong
I worry I can't take this anymore
I cry because it's been going on for so long
I am sorry I am weak
I understand now why you never cared
I say nothing, 'cause you're not worth the air
I dream that you were never there
I try not to think about the times we shared
I hope you know that I'm no longer scared
I am sorry I am weak

Sabrina A. Baker
Lycoming, NY

Romeo and Juliet

Romeo and Juliet
One might say
Kind of alike
In about one way
The love is like no other
A relationship so great
A bond that no one could break
I would do anything for you
You would do everything for me
I love you more than anyone
Can't you see?
If you left me
I would be lost forever
Roaming around
Carelessly free
Forgetting about everything
Reminding myself of you
I love you
Can't you see?
I love you more than anyone
Anywhere
The question for now
You don't love me?
How unfair

Blake E. Bartholomew
Rensselaer Falls, NY

Self-Diagnosis

Our Annie doesn't complain,
But she suddenly felt a mysterious pain.
Because of the urgency,
She went to emergency,
And they thought that she'd better remain.

She underwent all kinds of tests.
They wanted her to have the best.
After CAT scans and X-ray
Had all had their say,
They still couldn't explain
That mysterious pain.

Finally one morning she noticed a rash.
She sent for a doctor, who appeared in a flash.
Said she, "I think it's shingles, by heck."
Said he, "I think your hunch is correct."

Now it appears our pockets will jingle.
"Doctor" Annie will hang out her shingle!

William Belitz
Atlanta, GA

Conflict of Needs

I close my eyes and play my fingers along the peripheral of dreams
Too beautiful to be real.
Buried in the warmth of your arms
Breathing in the scent
Which I long to seep into my very being
Forever a memory should we ever be forced apart.
Knowing somewhere it could never be.
Deny my mind so my heart may soar.
I do not want to live in this cruel reality
If it means being without you.
Let me trace my fingers down the length of your spine.
Let me press my lips to your neck
And taste your skin.
I long for the fairy tale ending I was promised.
The fear of losing you completely keeps me from it.
But my body exists for your hands
My lips for your kiss.
My desires are for you alone.
Please bring my dreams to life.

Donna M. Chavez
Patchogue, NY

Childhood Memories

At night, I lay upon my bed,
And on my pillow, I rest my head.
Thoughts of childhood run through my mind,
Taking me back so far in time.
I think of my mother, a diamond in the rough.
From all her hard work, she grew up tough.
I think of my sisters and the fun we had,
And of all the hard times without a dad.
In winter, we hardly had shoes to wear.
Most all our clothes had lots of tears.
To the store we walked for miles.
We had no money for the latest styles.
Education was hard and cost so much.
School activities, we could not touch,
But we studied hard till late at night
For many years by a kerosene light.
Looking back over all my life,
For all I have, I've had to fight.
Most all those hardships are in the past.
I thank God every day some things never last.

Angela R. Beelier
Walton, KY

Alibis

She sat on a ledge,
lines of body straight.
Not to hesitate.
Alert and aware
if one cared.
Pretending not to be scared.
Head held high
with only a sigh.
Eyes closed to the truth.
Where is the root
of hate and lies?
Could it be our deceived eyes?
Carried away by lust.
Unable to trust.
But she must stand high
and only sigh,
aware she can only trust
her alibis.

Donna C. Cannon
Columbia, MS

I Feel As Though

I feel as though
I am looking in a
transparent mirror
You stripped away my identity
as a human being
I was defenseless
You were supposed
to cradle me and love me
Instead you could not show
anything but I can say
at least I am not stuck
in the shadow of your mistake
I beat to my own rhythm
You never got a chance
to know me as a person
Thank my lucky stars above
for giving me a reason to be here

Yvonne M. Sheret
Buffalo, NY

Frustration

So frustrated
So down and out
So frustrated
Give up or not
Sometimes I wonder
No friends
No love
So frustrated
I feel so alone in the place we call home
The world
So evil
So cold
I feel so alone
No one to talk to
Problems here
Problems there
Tears
Day in
Day out
So frustrated

Teanna T. Howard
Gainesville, FL

The Warrior

When you were in my arms as a child
Who knew that you had an inner strength?
I gave you the most important gift—that is life.
You are positively so bright!
As you were growing up, I hoped we would never be apart, my child,
But someone took you from my side.
That sadness in my heart, a parent couldn't hide.

Many were hoping for a miracle.
Thousands prayed, keeping their hearts with a psalm.
It became all too real when by surprise, by fortune,
A misfortune for many that could take an opportunity
From this situation.
Escaping from your captors in your homeland.
Thousands prayed for for your safe return.
The Lord granted us all the gift of hope and life.
Your striking brown eyes and skin soft as a rose.
You raised the expectations of yourself
In bringing courage to your heart.
Yes! Yes! I was right about you—you are a warrior!

Diana R. Gonzalez
Passaic, NJ

I was born in New York, New York. My parents are from Puerto Rico. This poem is
dedicated to people that have been freed from their captors, especially to I.B., who
was finally freed in an extraordinary rescue.

Hell Faded Away

Ain't no grave
Gonna hold my body down!
I know the man has the crown—
I won't be six feet under ground!

Ain't no grave
Gonna hold my body down!
I been dead once before—
Knocking on kingdom's door!

But ain't no grave
Gonna hold my body down!
I been shot with a gun,
And I'm the widow's seventh son!

I died on Christmas Day,
And Hell faded away,
Ain't no grave
Gonna hold this body down!

Earl C. Hightower
Hephzibah, GA

His Book

The brilliance of a setting sun,
The peace of a starlit night,
Blue skies and far horizons stretch
My mind and show His might.

But in His book, I find the thoughts
Of a risen, living, Lord;
Surely no wisdom can surpass
The wisdom written in His Word.

As I read, the spirit leads
Far from Man's distortions,
And into light by teaching me
Truth in precise portions.

I am convinced this book
Can loose anyone from the mire,
So as I go, may I study more
And never lose the desire.

Rosemary McGraw
Anderson, IN

Childhood in Appalachia

As a child in Appalachia, I would run and play
With other children every day.
What great fun we always had
As we played together, gals and lads!
In youth, I still had much fun
As we would race to see who could outrun.
After high school, I married and became a mom,
It was great pleasure from dark 'til dawn.
Today, I am a "GG," great-grandmom,
A pleasure I never want to run from.
Some tell me I am no longer a "spring chicken,"
I yell back at them, "I am still a-kickin!"
I may be old and outdated,
Yet I can do many things if I am outdated.
I can smile, joke, cook, see, and do much more,
I can play with children as long before.
Old age is how one looks at it,
Everyone grows older day by day, bit by bit.
My heart is as young as it was years ago,
I trust it will never grow old, no—never.

Louise H. Spencer
Louisville, KY

The Three and the Queen

The queen, the three, you look staring at me
and I am as worn as the stare on your face.
The three, you got the look of a mannequin,
the queen. Did I piece you together with my own hands?
I carefully place the crown on your head
with my kind hands and called you the queen.
The queen, I tell you, he is not real!
Will you understand if I told you?
His face looks like a mannequin but real.
Looks as if he was well put together by my kind hands.
The three, the queen, the look on your face is of my face.
The queen? In love I must!
The three, let's not waste time on that,
what we pieced together in our mind.
We did not piece each other together with our kind hands.
All of this about the mannequin look got me tied.
The queen, since we are seen,
the word "tired" is like never in me because I am the queen.
You placed the crown on my head
and called me the queen and you look
staring, as if it is love.

James E. Stowers
Yazoo City, MS

Flower Thoughts

Mother's flower gardens of long ago,
A variety of annuals each year,
Pansies, impatiens, petunias, more too;
My favorite, begonias, growing low.

A second garden in back of the house
Grew perennials, dahlias, lilies tall;
There were roses and sweet peas on a fence,
I even bought flowered cloth for a blouse!

Some flowers popular by our seasons;
Hepatica, tulips, lilacs in spring,
Poppies and snapdragons in summertime,
Mums bloom in the fall for many reasons.

It is amazing what comes from the sod.
Flowers are a beautiful gift from God.

Rowena S. Annunziato
Lancaster, NY

Paul Revere's Ride Revisited

Listen, my children, and don't you fear,
I'll tell the true story of Paul Revere.
You might have heard one a long time ago,
But the first guy who told it did not seem to know
Or else, for convenience, he chose at the time
To use ole Paul's name with its ready-made rhyme.
Longfellow's the cat who wrote the first tale
And the story he told must have kicked up a gale.
He got it all wrong, except for the horse,
Which did all the work, but got no credit, of course.
Paul started the ride like it said in Henry's tale,
But within twenty miles, they had him in jail.
What a problem that caused with the Redcoats around,
And the folks all asleep with no warning or sound,
But praise be to God that with no thought of fame,
A patriot stepped forth! Do you know his name?
He continued the ride and gave the alarm,
And the Minutemen mustered and kept us from harm.
Our country's great story is known far and wide,
But everyone thinks 'twas Paul made the ride
To give us the warning when he saw the light
And rouse up the folks as he rode through the night,
But 'twasn't Paul at all; that night-riding missile
Was really a dude named Israel Bissell.

Grady E. Griggs
Fayetteville, TN

The Others, They Came

They came to us on waves of wood,
And curiously on the shore we stood.
They gave us pretty things taken from their shoes,
But we took no notice we were being made of fools.
They present the Lord and His Savior Son,
And still no notice of our being undone.
Christianity was which we were to be converted,
With all our deities being subverted.
A gift was given, spread to every man, woman, child, and fox.
It was what people will call in a faraway time
The epidemic smallpox.
People by the hundreds fleeing from the afterlife
With sickness and death by their side,
But no matter how far they ran, there was no place they could hide.
Victory now set,
The others' plans could not be met.
The survivors were rounded up,
And we realized too late how much they had been corrupt.
First the lords and now the serfs,
Our land is what we trawl before the sun approaches first.
Backbreaking work is what we do 'til we can't stand.
We are no longer the Taino; people we are now Native American.
Set up in positions, we are the lowest of low,
And many see death as the only way to go.
With Man by the hour falling in exhaustion, never to awaken again,
We finally see what they did do and now what we can't.

Jasmine S. Stevenson
Brooklyn, NY

The Potter's Gem

The Potter took the clay
And said a prayer.
I will make a human
Who will be rare.
She will be Black
With much to say,
And will be used
In an altruistic way.
She will shine.
She will be the first of her kind,
And will keep in mind
Her ancestors of clay.
She will have pain,
But will use it
For others' gain
And give it a sublime aim.
She will be blessed
With good health and great wealth,
And not keep these blessings
For herself.
I will give her fame.
Oprah will be her name.
The world will not be the same.
Her love will be its gain.

Jessie L. Epps
Columbia, SC

Two Different Lovers

Dance with me
Twirling around this ballroom
An immortal and mortal
Vampire and human
Predator and prey
Two lovers dancing to a sweet swan serenade

Wishing to know your thoughts
To know many things
Making sure you're safe
Never have nor will another

Your cold touch
Against my warm skin
Your hard kiss
Against my soft lips

Holding one another close
Saying vows, first kiss of marriage
Knowing you love me
As me you
Slowly dance under the crescent moon
Two lovers bound for eternity

Michelle L. Priester
Pelion, SC

Hot Tears

His eyes filled with tears when he said
She died with her children around her bed
They came to see her on New Year's Eve
She was dying and they would not leave
They stayed with him long after her death
Grieving together following her last breath
The whole family slept in their small house
It didn't matter if it wasn't a penthouse
Her family had always been very close
Their visits were never overdose
Often they would go to babysit grandkids
Skipping parties so they could hug those kids
Now when he goes to bed and closes his eyes
He remembers her presence and softly cries
Life will never be quite the same
Now a widower calling out his wife's name
As he sits down to read the cards again
Hot tears roll down his cheeks and then
He remembers how his family came to his side
And wipes away those hot tears with pride

Leonard R. Capuano
Barnegat, NJ

The loss of a spouse is one of the most devastating of life's events. When my friend's wife died, he described her death and subsequent events to me with much emotion. His love and devotion to her was very apparent. His family provided great comfort and support during this trying time. While I never met her, I wanted to describe this sad occasion in verse. The family was so touched and appreciative that they read this poem at her memorial service.

Dear Patience

I am really angry with the
lessons you keep giving out.
Frustration is exploding in my mind and
my tears are shouting, "Enough already!"
The tests you give are not so nice either,
for you often give them without any warning,
and why do you insist on giving me the same
test over and over?
Why can't you let me pass with a "C"?
Why do you expect more out of me than all the others?
Patience, you appear rude at times,
for you often show up without
being invited, like a thunderstorm
awaking me out of a sound sleep.
Oh, patience!
Pity me, pity me.
Why are you so hard on me?
And although I know you should be a part
of my character, I don't know if we
will ever be friends.
I don't know if I really trust you,
for if I let you into my heart,
what will I receive in return?

Rhonda J. Dalton
Woodridge, NY

Flesh

He touches her flesh,
Soft but just full of lust.
There is no devotion in his eyes,
And for as long as she has known,
It has not mattered.
Love has evaded her,
How it is not meant to be hard,
And soft kisses can fill voids.
He touches her low now,
Opening her thighs,
But he will not kiss her.
Taking her body,
Filling it with his own,
She still does not know love.
As moans escape her lips,
She is satisfied in this moment,
But she knows there is no magic,
There is no love,
And she does not care.

Lauren R. Kessler
Staughton, MA

Table of Life

Come on and drink you who are thirsty
Come on and eat you who are hungry
And be filled from the table of life.

Drink from the fountain of living water
Eat the bread of His living Word
Be a partaker and worship at the altar
Worship and glorify Jesus Christ, our Lord.

He filled me and healed me
He's the reason I must go on
He picked me up from the miry clay
I became a new creature on that great day.

Now my life is sweeter even in sorrow
Tonight I weep, but joy comes tomorrow
My thirst is quenched, my hunger is fed
I am filled from the table of life.

Rosa H. Carroll
Troy, AL

I was very shy as a youth. Through life's experiences as an adult, the love of writing was a way of self-expression and giving God praise for keeping me through my battles and victories. I am awakened in the night and prompted by the Holy Spirit to write poems and sometimes just writings of encouragement, which I share with many others along life's journey.

Homeward

Crimson hem of fading light
touches blackness.
Wintering trees stand like soldiers,
silently waiting,

watching a nameless star's rising
brilliantly points me home
after day is done,
enough stuff fills my head

until I hear
the wordless whisper cleans the slate,
my mind, preoccupied.
I now can hear, truly.

Watched from afar by a star
I stare at this masterpiece aglow
and know
Bethlehem opens doors,
even to the lost, crushed, keyless,
locked out from inside.
Crimson light finds entrance.

Martine H. Otto
Center Valley, PA

Seniors

What can we say about our seniors of this day
That quite possibly may deter our youth from going astray?
Being a senior myself, I feel that much can be said
That can help our youth to stand in their own stead
The bottom line, quite frankly,
Is we must start training from the cradle
To mould our youth in life so that in time
They will be able
To cope with life's trials, no matter the cost,
So that in the end, nothing's lost
When our youths reach the age of consent,
We as seniors can feel that our efforts were well spent
Not all of our youths may excel in life,
But hopefully our teachings help them to avoid much strife
We seniors who are inclined to do the right thing
Will ultimately get to meet the great King.

Milton C. Plummer
New Carrollton, MD

Timeslot

Still life day seems
Sunlit midnight
Keen Canada geese
Seek out in the sky
Expanse of the space
Flapping rhythm dynamize
Innate urge to unravel
Eternity's time domain
Cool subway streams
Winding silk strand
Calligraphy clouds kiss
Opaque blue of hills
Silence resonates
Unheard of strains of
"Viola d'amore"!

Amit Sarkar
Westwood, MA

Tears of a Clown

As I put this paint on my face like a shield,
Maybe the world won't see my tears
As I entertain your child,
Inside trying to keep myself from going wild!
As I see all of the smiles,
Feeling empty as all the people applaud.
Solving people problems with my many skills,
But when I am alone, there are many tears.
As I bring the people so much joy,
I feel so mach pain!
The tears of a clown hit my soul like rain!
The darkness on my heart is like a bad stain.
I made a lot of money but it's hard to maintain.
The tears of a clown!
It's off to a new city
As I think back to the beginning.
Should've taken the job as the ring leader!

Gordon Franklin
Warren, OH

The Ballad of a Cupid's Arrow

I saw an archer, his bow up-raised,
An arrow notched and firmly settling.
His left hand pushed away the bow,
Holding the bowstring.
I glimpsed a rivulet of light
That limned the golden crafted arrow,
Gleaming along the trembling shaft
Spanning his torso;
And then I saw in one brief moment
The archer, bow, arrow, and target
Froze into one unconscious whole.
All senses quit;
Gloved fingers let the bowstring slip
To let the feathered arrow fly.
The shaft looses itself, a mote
To the human eye.
Heard the fluted flight, faint as a wing-beat
Of some swift bird . . . the arrow's gone,
And the thwack of the bamboo turned the bow
In the shooter's hand.
Saw the shot continued, the follow-through,
The archer, unmoving in hypnotic track,
The un-glimpsed arrow embedded itself,
Its true mark struck!

Edmundo C. Lozada
New York, NY

Dreams

Everyday life is certainly rough.
Sometimes getting through days is just too tough.
Having special dreams of what could be now,
some dreams are goals we can reach if we knew how.

Everyone has ideas of what matters most,
you hear it from voices from coast to coast.
Most want more money, a home, or love,
some want peace and goodwill on wings of a dove.

Dreams take us places we just can't get to,
changes are endless, every day something new.
Think of your dreams, what they mean to you,
how you can change things to make some come true.

Always remember, all dreams are within reach,
some inspiring us so we may teach.
Take chances on your dreams a time or two,
the path you're on now could all be brand-new.

Lisa J. Boisvert
Charlton, MA

To My Beloved William

When I fall asleep,
all I can see is your face
All I can taste
are your lingering, gentle kisses
All I can feel is your tender
fingertips caressing me so . . .
then I awake to find an empty
bed and I'm alone for the day
with nothing to think of but you
and all the happiness and joy that
you have brought into my life
It is your presence and essence
that makes my heart yearn for
every second that we are not together
It is your charming smile and your
laughter worth every waking moment
And now, it will be you and our
daughter that makes every moment
worth living.

Crystal L. Bradford
Woodsville, NH

The Edge

2009

Time is of the essence,
Essence, I fear my homeland has been ransomed.
Ransomed with eyes of our nation closed shut,
Shut to my small meek voice fading off.
Off in the distance unheard by ears slammed closed,
Closed to keep our America safe and sound,
Sound as the foundation "we, the people" was built on.
On the wings of our nation, shall our words soar,
Soar onward to set the checks and balances?
Balances wavered on the tilted scale,
Scales of time are weighed unbalanced.
Unbalanced truths hope to level their way straight,
Straight to keep our American strong,
Strong should be our freedoms in our capitalist America.
America gives us the right to choose,
Choose to vote, to make our nation right.
Right to wave our red, white, and blue flag,
Flag of our nation, fly high, stand tall, be proud.
Proud to be our capitalist America,
America, America is the foundation forever,
Forever let freedom be this nation.

Carol A. Scarofile Krause
Orange, MA

Winter

Trees with bare wings
Etchings in the sky

Beautiful, fanciful creations
Of the artist from on high

Who looks upon the Earth
And decorates it with beauty

With a touch of the Almighty
Transforming the lush of summer
Into the intricate artistry of winter

Snowflakes dancing in the wind
Jewels rare from the Master's hand

Transforming the Earth
Into a fairyland

Mildred Spencer
Corbin, KY

Remember Me

Run to the beach
My dear friend
My footprints
Are buried there
Somewhere
Long ago
There was a me
Someone
You will never see
Buried by the sea
Like shattered shells
Along the shore
Discarded memories
Nothing more
Pounding surf
Echoes my name
Never the same . . . .

Donna J. Shaver
Laurens, NY

The Storm

The branches obedient to the voice of the wind
Swag back and forth
And the tree shakes as gentle tears
Wash over him
The Earth's mouth opens wide
Drinking until she is full
Now storm clouds like a waring army
March through the heavens
Crushing the tiny clouds
They etch out their countenance
The rain heavy beats upon the ground
Under its weight her heart sinks deep
Lighting lifts his sword
As his steed moves fast
And fire dances across the sky
Searching where to strike
Fear rattles the tree
He lays low and waits
Until the storm is over.

Joanne Hebb Panzarella
Lakeland, FL

You Thought Me into Your Life

You made me in the center of your every thought
Toward me, are good for me and not evil.
From the height of the highest sky
To the floor of the deepest sea,
I don't have to have time from You to steal,
And I don't have to ask the question why,
For You know my every action,
And you know my every reaction.
My thoughts are overwhelmed
By the care You give me, by Your outstretched arms.
I never have the need to fear alarm,
You care for me in every season under the sun.
You lead me and guide me
By Your light shining through me.
You wrote me into life with Your every thought.
You formed every part of me.
Like a book, You have opened me,
And have read every word you have formed in me,
In the corner of Your thoughts toward me.
From Heaven up above,
You thought me into life by Your abounding love.

Clifford J. Seab
Chattanooga, TN

Other Mothers

Memories become so precious when Mother's Day draws near,
But there are other mothers who never get any cheer.

They bottle-fed the babies and changed their diapers too,
And later on they dressed them and sent them off to school.

They fried your favorite apple pies and baked your favorite dish,
And when you came back from the lake, they even cleaned your fish.

Who is this other mother who never gets any attention
And whose name is never mentioned?

It is none other than our mother-in-laws that we are talking about,
So let's stand up and praise them and give them a shout.

Berta D. Cook
Graham, NC

At age seventy-five, I am visually impaired. It was a blessing to start writing poetry. Since then, I have written many poems, but this particular poem speaks for itself. Many poems and songs have been written about mothers, but often mothers-in-law are the brunt of jokes and not appreciated. Hopefully this poem will cause readers to realize what a blessing a mother-in-law can be.

The Abyss

The dark greets me.
I hear the shadows call,
Teasing, tormenting, taunting.
It wants to consume me.
I will not give in;
It held me once,
Cloying, choking.
But I broke free once—
And once the darkness holds you,
It does not give up.
It seethes at my escape,
Angry at my freedom.
I hear it whisper,
"You are mine, forever,
No one else can have you!
No one can free you!"
But I am free, I freed myself.
Yet I feel the darkness,
I see the abyss before me—
And a face, twisted, dark, evil;
My face stares back at me.

Laura E. Misciasci
Fremont, OH

The Power of the Lord

I stood afar
to look upon
the cross
where Jesus died

Tears fell
and mixed
with crimson blood
I bowed my head
and cried

And lo'
a rushing sound
I heard
'twas not of any wind
but the Power of the Lord
His blood consumed my sin

Alas
my Savior
called my name
I mounted up on golden wings
to meet Him
in the sky

Sonya M. Davis
Hampton, VA

I am a seventh grade English teacher and I have taught for twenty-seven years. I've always loved words and the thought of putting them together to make beautiful poetry is what I have always enjoyed doing. I wrote my first words when I was five and I have been writing ever since. My goal and purpose is to glorify God. He gives me the beautiful words to write. When I read them, I smile and say "God, you are awesome." And He is! I have three daughters and three grandchildren who are the loves of my life.

Upliftment

My beloved is mine and I am his
I lay me my head his hairy chestnut chest
With quaking, quivering hands, yearning, agonized in dreary depths
Longing anew a grip strong and sedulous
Lovingly, his shaking arms wrap around
My yoked beaded bouncing bowls
A revival awakening surge through me
Birthing an unquenchable, zealous zone.

My beloved is mine and I am his
I tiptoed, me aside his strong stony stature
With wavering, wobbling feet; groaning, engulfed in panicking pains
Pleading again a lift pure and powerful
Carefully he stood solid still
My brittle, broken bones abased
A bright, brilliant blend beseeching my marrow
Rising with uncontrollable ardor

My beloved is mine and I am his
I stealthily crawled, strayed aside his sage-scented section
With mumbling murmuring lips moaning, tormented in fiery fire
Searching afresh a touch solemn and serene
Silently, his soothing lips reached out
My contoured curvature caressed
A simultaneous overflow of sensations flew
Beaming with inexplicable ecstasy

Diana V. Sey
Worcester, MA

Crosses

In Normandy, if you go
You'll see crosses row on row
Those were people, this we know
Long forgotten until now

They were human like we are
But their life did not go far
Given up for stripe and star
In a land from home afar

Anniversaries give us thought
Those were men who here fought
But they died when live they ought
And thus our freedom they bought

But do we them now honor
All the things they fought for
No, we still wage unjust war
And plant crosses as before

Charles J. Fickey
Silver Spring, MD

My Struggle

Lord, Jesus, Thou hast given me a burden
And Thou hast promised not more than I can bear.
I feel the ground beneath me crumble
And sense disaster in the air.
Please touch me, Lord, and strengthen me
That I may have no fear.

Keep me walking in Thy footsteps
And I'll hold tight my Savior's hand,
For He will guide me through this tempest
And bring me safely to dry land.

I worship Thee, Lord Jesus Christ,
Thy holy blood has washed me clean.
I look forward to the rapture
And Heaven's eternal and glorious scene.

David L. Owen
New Portland, ME

Magnificent Clouds

Clouds appear fragile, made of fluff and light,
But are garments to bind waters with their might.
He gives this blessing to each coming generation,
They also adorn Heaven; what a decoration!
Of all shapes and sizes, yet balanced to swing,
They dance and swirl to the bidding of the King.

At sundown, many clouds change their complexion.
When throw back of sunrays cast a reflection,
It creates a glow, and they wear a blush of pink,
With storm clouds wearing blue, some dark as ink.
Beautiful white clouds keep drifting on by
In the huge bowl of azure blue sky.

Clouds hold rainbows, a promise after rain,
That water won't destroy us, not ever again.
God uses clouds as a chariot to glide or descend,
He'll break through the blue in one, come the end.
His shout, "Come up hither," will cause us to rise
To meet our dear Savior in azure blue skies.

Edith V. Gray
Lehigh Acres, FL

Dove in Hand

Dove in hand, he did not cease the moment.
Up above lurking in the dark, a eagle in flight,
Waiting for the right moment to scoop up the dove in hand,

Left unattended. Wings spread like an eagle,
He eyes the dove, with so much love, that soon
She'll be his for the taking.

He leaves the darkness of the night and circles the sky,
With the brightness of the moon,
Making images and shadows on the lake below.
Eagled eyes watching intently through the winded skies,
He soars the love he admires from up above,
That will soon be his.

Once again the dove in hand. They say they care,
Their minds have wondered leaving the beautiful dove in hand
Under-nourished, unattended.
The time is right, the eagle is in flight.
Down from the clouds he flies

To me the dove.

Claws as sharp as knives,
He pierces the heart of the dove with his love,
Scoops the beauty into his feathered chest
And flies to the mountaintop,
Where is hidden a nest he has prepared for the beautiful dove.

When you are left unattented,
You leave the destiny of the dove to the eagle in flight.

Judy Soto
Paradise, CA

A Continuity of Gulbenkians' Family

This is a continuity of the last year's poem about the Gulbenkians'
Family, an unusually excellent family who came and left this world
like by a thunder being wiped out, the unique philanthropists.

My sister's two sons, Stefan and John-Sarkis.
Stefan's two sons, Christopher and Gary, and John-Sarkis's sons,
Alexander and Michael Yerganians, inferred that they were
Gulbenkians' granddaughter's, Haigouhi's granddaughter's
Elisa's sons and grandsons.

Gulbenkians, a wealthy family in Kaiseri, who indiscriminately helped
people of any creed or nationality and posterities are continuing.

My cousin in Canada, Marie Terryan, her father Sebouh,
who was a brother of my grandmother, Haigouhi.
Marie's two sons, Dane and Terry, got very proud
and happy to be Gulbenkians' grandson's grandsons.

My mother's sister's son, Levon Markarian, in Athens, Greece,
his son, Carlos, Carlos's son, Angelo, Levon's daughters, Ilenia and
Norita, Ilenia's son, Leonida, were very glad
to be Gulbenkians' grandchildren

People know the orphanages, hospitals, schools that they had built,
the donations of millions of dollars
in Asia Minor in 1938 and 1939 for the earthquakes
by Kaloust Gulbenkian.

Louise Ajemian
Astoria, NY

To My Mother

Oh, how I love her,
I could never put anyone above her,
and I'm so sorry I ever
disrespected
'cause I see how it affected
my life and my dear mother's.
Oh, yeah, happy birthday.
Without tomorrow, the twenty-ninth of November,
I'd never endeavor
the life in which I presume.
I'm glad I have her living in the next room.
Without her I'd be living in a jail-doom
going crazy.
Thanks to her, I'm kicking it, being lazy,
and I'm so thankful for my moms.
She belongs in the Book of Psalms.
Her heart is made of gold.
My love for her can never grow cold.
I love her so much it can hurt,
but only when I desert
the things she has raised in me to believe,
so now I must go and retrieve
the virtues that good old Moms
has instilled from the start.
The day of her birth, I truly take to heart.

Pat Geise
Ojai, CA

What Is One to Do?

I'm sorry, please know I love you
I hate to see your pain
You've got nothin' to lose,
Everything to gain
Put it in your pocket,
Never to be taken out again
Roll it around with your change
Act like it will spend
Or stomp a mud hole in it and walk it a day
Because you can't hide from it
That would just be a lie
Broke my last 100 this morning
Don't know where the next one is coming from
Even spending money has grown old
What am I gonna do
Got to have money to live
Guess I'll go back to work
If I can find a job that gives
Love, hugs, prayers, and a smile is all you need
Like to look in your eyes for a while
Deep, dark, and blue
I'm so sorry
Please know that I love you

Tony McKinney
Steinhatchee, FL

The Holding

Hold me,
take me in your arms.
Let me feel your warmth.
Hold me,
embrace me with your heart.
Let me know your love.
Hold me
till my trembling ends.
Let me hear your sigh.
Hold me,
breathe within my joy.
Let me feel your caress.
Hold me
till the longing leaves my heart.
Let me feel your kiss.
Hold me,
take my breath away.
Let me know your passion.
Hold me
till I feel safe,
and then . . . hold me!

Ed Banks
Mauldin, SC

Mask

A mask can hide anything one wants.
You paint one on every morning.
The mask can hide, but the pain still haunts.
It will be a constant warning.

It will be there when you get home.
It will even be in your dreams,
Keeping you awake, making you roam.
The pain won't go, it seems.

And yet you continue to paint the mask.
A pretty smile even looks genuine.
Hiding the truth can be quite a task.
Some will be able to see through to the ruin.

And when alone, the mask will finally be gone,
Revealing the obvious pain and sorrow.
You will be naked, ugly, and feeling done
Until you put the mask on again tomorrow.

April Alvear
Owings Mills, MD

I believe poetry is a way for our feelings to be let out. Poetry has been a big help to me and I love to express myself through it. It doesn't have to be good or bad, it just has to be you.

INDEX OF POETS

E

F

D

W

Y

Z

Breinigsville, PA USA
13 April 2010
235995BV00002B/2/P